JOURNEY TO ILLUSTRATION & COMIC BOOK DESIGN

College Admissions & Profiles

Rachel A. Winston, Ph.D.

Lizard Publishing is not sponsored by any college. While data was derived by school, state, or nationally published sources, some statistics may be out of date as published sources vary widely based upon the date of submission and currency of numbers. Attempts were made to obtain the best information during the writing of this book from, NCES, U.S. Census Bureau, U.S. Department of Education, Common Data Set, College Board, U.S. News & World Report, college, and organizational sites. Descriptions of colleges are a compilation of college website information as well as student, faculty, and staff interviews with individuals and often from unique experiences and impressions. Attempts were made to triangulate multiple points of light. If you would like to share program information, data, or an impression of a specific college, please write to Lizard Publishing at the address below or at the e-mail address: *collegeguide@yahoo.com*

ISBN 978-1946432735 (hardback); 978-1946432728 (paperback); 978-1946432742 (e-book)

LCCN: 2022907969

Lizard Publishing, 7700 Irvine Center Drive, Suite 800, Irvine, CA 92618 *www.lizard-publishing.com*

Lizard Publishing creates, designs, produces, and distributes books and resources to provide academic, admissions, and career information. Our mental process is fueled by three tenets:

- Ignite the hunger to learn and the passion to make a difference
- Illuminate the expanse of knowledge by sharing cutting edge thinking
- Innovate to create a world that makes the transition from dreams to reality

We work with academic leaders who transform the educational landscape to publish relevant content and advise students of their educational and professional options, with the aim of developing 21st-century learners and leaders. We also work with students to publish their books and present widely diverse ideas to the college/graduate school-bound community. With headquarters in Irvine, California, Lizard Publishing works virtually with authors to edit, publish, and distribute both hard copy and paperback books.

This book was published in the U.S.A. Lizard Publishing is a premium quality provider of educational reference, career guidance, and motivational publications/merchandise for global learners, educators, and stakeholders in education.

Book design by Michelle Tahan *www.michelletahan.com*

Book formatting by Obinna Chinemerem Ozuo

Book website: *www.collegelizard.com*

LIZARD PUBLISHING

This book is dedicated to Amber Levitt, who epitomizes dedication, multi-dimensional talent, and professionalism.

ACKNOWLEDGMENTS

There is never enough room to acknowledge every person. Numerous people contributed to my perspective about art. Students, faculty, counselors, and researchers assisted in enhancing my knowledge base or taught me indelible lessons. Over a lifetime of experiences working with students, I am wiser and more worldly.

I gratefully acknowledge Michelle Tahan, Jasmine Jhunjhnuwala, E. Liz Kim, and Jacqueline Xu, as well as my family, friends, colleagues, and professors. With profound gratitude, I also acknowledge those I have known in the art world.

As a faculty member in the UCLA College Counseling Certificate Program, I met many dedicated counselors who spend their life serving and supporting students. Meaningful contributions to the book have been made indirectly by admissions representatives, college counselors, and faculty members who took a special interest in this book's success.

I would also like to thank the thousands of students I have taught, counseled, or supported in my nearly four decades of service.

> *"If I see so far, it is because I stand on the shoulders of giants."*
> *Isaac Newton*

Isaac Newton once said, "If I see so far, it is because I stand on the shoulders of giants." A few of those giants whose broad shoulders lifted me higher and helped teach invaluable lessons include Madison May, Julian Falagan, Eddie Gallardo, Hannah Heydorff, Chloe Grubb, Cecilia Yang, Katie Foose, Julianne Alfe, Shea Harris, Sarve Khorramshahi, Marissa Kotch, Stefy Lin, Barien Gad, Sammy Seefeldt, and Sabrina Wang.

Finally, there would be no book on illustration and comic art schools and no career college admissions counseling without the support of Robert Helmer, whose tireless efforts support me every single day.

ABOUT THE AUTHOR

D r. Rachel A. Winston is a tireless student advocate. She has served the educational community as a university professor, college advisor, statistician, researcher, author, cryptanalyst, motivational speaker, publishing executive, and lifelong student. As one of the leading experts in college counseling and an award-winning faculty member, Dr. Winston has spent her lifetime learning, teaching, mentoring, and coaching students. Her counseling practice centers around college admissions, college essays, portfolios, and intellectual conversations about life and career pursuits.

She started college at thirteen and graduated from college programs in such widely ranging disciplines as chemistry, mathematics, computers, liberal arts, international relations, negotiation, conflict resolution, peacebuilding, business administration, higher education leadership, interpreting, college counseling, and publishing. Throughout her education, she attended and graduated from Harvard, University of Chicago, University of Texas, GWU, UCLA, Syracuse, CSUF, CSUDH, Pepperdine, Claremont Graduate University, and Gallaudet University.

Her position working in Washington, D.C. on Capitol Hill and with the White House in the 1980s took her to approximately a hundred universities training campaign managers at colleges from Colorado to California, thoroughly dotting the western states. Later, she led college tours with students and their families on road trips throughout the United States. She has taught or counseled thousands of students over her career and speaks at conferences and academic programs throughout the world.

As a professor and avid writer for numerous publications, she won the 2012 McFarland Literary Achievement Award, Bletchley Park Cryptanalyst Award, and numerous other awards, including Faculty Member of the Year, Leadership Tomorrow Leader of the Year, and college service and leadership awards. While studying Human Capital at Claremont Graduate University, she was a scholarship recipient at the Drucker School of Management. She was also elected to the statewide Board of Governors for the Faculty Association for California Community Colleges, where she served on their executive committee.

She also served as a faculty member for the UCLA College Counselor Certificate Program, the Director of Mathematics at Brandman University, and Embry Riddle Aeronautical University, Chapman University, Cal State Fullerton, and a handful of California Community Colleges, including Cerro Coso College where she represented the entire faculty as the Academic Senate President and retired in 2016. Over her career, she taught mathematics online, on television, live interactive satellite, telecourses, and in large and small lecture halls.

AUTHOR'S NOTE

You are reading this book because you are considering admission to colleges where you open the doors to the world of art, design, and creativity. Whatever route you took to get to this point, you are in the right place. Right now, you need to gather information to make informed decisions.

While many people offer advice, suggestions differ. Friends will tell you the 'right' way or the way their neighbor was accepted. Graciously accept this anecdotal information, pursuing imaginative artistry with your heart and mind as you commit to learning more.

Dig deeper to consider both expert and current information from counselors who have worked with hundreds of students. Changes in programs, curricula, requirements, and links happen each year.

Doublecheck each program's specifics yourself. Each school's profile information is current as of April 2022. However, since researching this book, changes may have taken place. There are other college guidebooks written by talented and experienced counselors, though none like this book on college programs for illustration, cartooning, and comic book design.

> *"We are what we think. All that we are arises with our thoughts. With our thoughts, we make the world."*
> — *Buddha*

This book, providing lists of colleges, admissions information, and profiles, is different in that it also offers unique tidbits. I hope you find the information valuable. Your job is to begin early by assembling lists of possible schools to consider. Create a road map and set yourself on a clear path.

If you see an error in this book or even a suggestion for a future edition, please write to Dr. Rachel A. Winston at collegeguide@yahoo.com. We will fix the entry with the next printed version. All of that said, this book was written with you in mind.

This book contains a wealth of information on the Internet with free downloads, FAQs, testimonials, and offers to help you with your applications. Some of these advisors are knowledgeable and provide valuable assistance. Unfortunately, students and parents hunt around the web, searching for a tremendous number of hours to seek the information they need. This book aims to resolve this problem with college admissions data and profiles to make your search easier.

For now, though, I will assume you want to attend college to study illustration and comic book design and are exploring this book to find a program that will get you on your way toward your goal. You are undoubtedly a talented candidate who is willing to work very hard. Creative mental exploration is virtually a prerequisite for all art programs.

As you investigate colleges, you might find that some programs are listed in different college departments. Either way, this book will help you reach your goal. Applying to and writing essays for each application will require research to determine which program is right for you and the specific reasons you are a good fit.

While you might believe that art-focused colleges are relatively similar, each program's nuances make them very different. These small differences may seem confusing. My goal with this book is to demystify the information and process.

CONTENTS

CHAPTER 1

CAPTURING PEOPLE'S IMAGINATION: CREATING CHARACTERS AND TELLING STORIES

"When Superman came out it galvanized the entire industry. It's just part of the American scene. Superman is going to live forever. They'll be reading Superman in the next century when you and I are gone."

– Jack Kirby

A dream you dream alone is only a dream. A dream you dream together is reality.

– Yoko Ono

VISUAL STORYTELLING

One of the greatest joys in inspirational storytelling is the ability to empower and motivate others through your words and art. At the same time, you pursue a passion you love so deeply that you would immerse yourself wholeheartedly. This joy is not elusive. You can train in specialized character building and digital design skills and then translate the messages you want to convey to your audience through stories. Sir Terry Pratchett author of the 41-book "Discworld" fantasy series said, "If we spend life's precious days intentionally unearthing our own greatest talents, passions, and abilities, happiness will follow where they lead."

Illustrators and comic book artists can achieve their dreams through humor. In this way, the world can laugh at life and move forward with hope or a thought-provoking idea. We can take the oddities in life and look at them in a slightly different way, possibly with a moral message or possibly with a dystopian question mark about the world's future. We might just find the idea so funny we simply laugh. Greats in this field came before you to illuminate your path like Scott Adams, the creator of the *Dilbert* comic strip, Nicholas Gurewitch, the creator of *The Perry Bible Fellowship* comic, Gary Larson, creator of *The Far Side*, and Bob Mankoff, Cartoon Editor for The New Yorker. Interestingly, Gary Larson is the only cartoonist to receive a Pulitzer Prize for a comic strip.

Beginning with a vision and a sketch, a lightning bolt appears. Drums begin to crescendo until the clouds part and the sun shines on a previously obscured path. In dramatic form, the darkness disappears, and surprises show up offering you the power to share your talent and uplift the lives of others in unknowing ways. An illustrator is more than a person who can draw. Most illustrators have deep thoughts and profound ideas they want to convey. These beliefs, reflections, and visions lay with creative imagery.

Art is just the beginning. Stories lurk behind every artwork or character. Live fully. Share selflessly.

You only get one life.

The only calibration that counts is how much heart people invest, how much they ignore their fears of being hurt or called out or humiliated. And the only thing people regret is that they didn't live boldly enough, that they didn't invest enough heart, didn't love enough. Nothing else really counts at all.

- Ted Hughes (1930 – 1998)

While some comic and cartoon artists spread humor and fun in society, many sowed seeds of political change. James Thurber (1894 – 1961) was one of those who included both humor and thoughtful societal awareness. World War I began in 1914, when Thurber was twenty years old. Thurber attended Ohio State University before taking posts in the U.S. Department of State in Washington, D.C. and then Paris. He worked with *The Columbus Dispatch*, *Chicago Tribune*, *New York Evening Post*, and *The New Yorker* writing articles and cartoons, reminding people, "Let us not go back in anger or forward in fear, but around in awareness." His work inspired the Thurber Prize for American Humor. He cautioned, "Don't let past disappointments color how you see the world. When entering any situation, assuming the worst suspends our ability to access authentic emotions, and, as a result, few clear-eyed, open-hearted decisions are made."

Stepping farther from humor and more into social awareness, cartoonists and comic strip artists can highlight numerous issues in a way that cannot be done otherwise.

"A Graphic Sentence" – Plantu, 2006

"Don't Waste Petrol. It Costs Lives" – Philip Zec, 1942

"Rendezvous" – Sir David Low, 1939

"Germany Shall Never Be Encircled" – E.H. Shepard, 1939

"Tattooed Man" – Bernard Gillam, 1884

"Who Store the People's Money?" / "Twas Him," – Thomas Nast, 1871

"A Scene on the Frontiers as Practiced by the 'Humane' British and their 'Worthy Allies'" – William Charles, 1812

"The Plumb-Pudding in Danger – Or – State Epicures Taking Un Petit Souper" – James Gillray, 1805

"The Abolition of the Slave Trade – Or – The Inhumanity of Dealers in Human Flesh" – Isaac Cruikshank, 1792

"Join, or Die" – Benjamin Franklin, 1754

EXPOSING GRIM REALITIES

One image reveals naked realities, exposing life as it appears. *Time* magazine released a list of one hundred of the most impactful pictures ever taken.[1] Similar to powerfully moving cartoons and illustrations, some photographs will never be forgotten, including the terror of the Vietnam war, the self-immolation of Buddhist monks, "Flag Raising at Mt. Suribachi", "Tank Man", and "Mushroom Cloud over Nagasaki". These images will live on, forever etched in our memories.

Time editors explained, *"The best photography is a form of bearing witness, a way of bringing a single vision to the larger world."* The adage "a picture is worth a thousand words" is never truer than in the hundred images *Time* selected.

Early use of that phrase appeared in a 1918 *San Antonio Light*, newspaper,

One Picture is Worth a Thousand Words
The San Antonio Light's Pictorial Magazine of the War
Exemplifies the truth of the above statement.[2]

ILLUMINATING SOCIAL CONDITIONS THROUGH ART

While bombs, genocide, torture, poverty, famine, slavery, depression, and disease highlight some of our local and global problems, art can bring to

---

1 Ben Goldberger. 2016. "Most Influential Photos." *Time*, November 17, 2016. https://time.com/4574500/most-influential-photos/

2 "Pictorial Magazine of the War (advertisement)". *San Antonio Light*. January 10, 1918. p. 6.

light numerous other challenges and instantaneously share them with people throughout the world. We cannot be everywhere simultaneously and cannot truly comprehend the lived experiences of humanity through words or a picture, but we can come closer to grasping its impact.

People clamor to fathom uncertainties that complicate their lives like political strife, new technologies, environmental hazards, food security, and the impacts of inflation. With a tsunami of sociocultural transformation, overwhelming evidence portends dynamic change on the horizon. This one moment is an exciting and possibly harrowing juncture. You can make a difference by recognizing, analyzing, and capturing images of what is happening today. College academic programs offer a myriad of ways to view the challenges and seek new opportunities by designing next-gen possibilities.

A FEW FACTS TO CONSIDER

1. The COVID-19 pandemic impacted people globally with more than six million deaths.
2. Africa's population is expected to double by 2050.
3. Supply chains, transportation mechanisms, and limiting factors of non-renewable resources threaten populations.
4. Oceans are dying due to overfishing, pollution, and climate change.
5. With the melting of the Arctic and Antarctic, many islands and cities are likely to be partially underwater by 2050.

6. According to NOAA, Miami's sea level is 8 inches higher now than in 1950.

7. Global angst, propaganda mechanisms, and philosophical divisions threaten to widen the fissure between people.

8. According to the UN, one in three people globally do not have adequate access to food.

9. World Bank data show that nearly ten percent of the world survives day to day on less than $1.90.

10. Inflation and financial crises increased uncertainty since the end of the pandemic.

Winston Churchill stated, "Those who fail to learn from history are doomed to repeat it." While solving today's problems, we hold images in our memory, allowing us to see what appears in front of us while observing what we intend to act upon and change. As Mahatma Gandhi explained in 1913, that change in the world must start within since we are but a mirror in the world. As we change our nature, the world's attitude also changes in a divine mystery that stems from the source of our happiness. We can change the world, one image, cartoon, or story at a time.

Think lightly of yourself and deeply of the world.

– Miyamoto Musashi, A Famed Japanese Swordsman

ORIGINS OF COMIC BOOK ART

Swiss comic book artist, Rodolphe Töpffer (1799 – 1846) is credited with inventing the comic book strip. A scholarly chronology of comic strip history appearis in a two-volume tome by UCLA professor emeritus David Kunzle.[3] While not all comic strips were humorous, they all had illustrations and a storyline. Some art historians focus their research on caricatures, political illustrations, comics, presenting their findings at conferences and in articles. You, too, might find this history fascinating, particularly the graphic novel *The Picturesque, Dramatic, and Caricatural History of Holy Russia* (1854) which contained five hundred drawings. This piece, containing anti-Russian propaganda by Gustave Doré, presented graphic images and caricatures corresponding to European hostility toward Russia.

In 1829, one year before the Revolution (not the French Revolutions of 1789 or 1848), political relations between France and Switzerland soured Honoré-Victorin Daumier "the Michelangelo of Caricature" (1808 – 1879) and Jean Ignace

---

3 David Kunzle, *History of the Comic Strip,* 2 vols. (Berkeley and Los Angeles: University of California Press, 1973–90)

Isidore Gérard Grandville, known as J. J. Grandville (1803 – 1847) were prolific French caricaturists. Presenting mostly political caricatures that were sometimes charming and other times disquieting, they made a mark on society, which provided an oppositionist viewpoint.

Charles Amédée de Noé, also known as Cham (1818 – 1879) was a famous French caricaturist, illustrator, and cartoonist. He satirized politics and society. He was a prolific illustrator with more than 4,000 drawings. Some of his elements of humor and techniques in cartooning are still used today. Cham never cut his aristocratic ties, though he did not follow the 'correct' path of the son of a count. Gustave Doré (1832 – 1883), another French illustrator, comic artist, caricaturist, sculptor, and printmaker followed in Cham's footsteps, illustrating classic books, including the Bible. The list of his notable works seems endless.

In the 1900s, satirical, political, motivational, and humorous illustrations, caricatures, and comic books emerged with a wider array of artists and storytellers. With the wars of the early 1900s people either read comic strips or comic books to cast their worries away or to view the wars from a socio-political perspective. While fewer people read comic books today, decades ago, they were the staple medium for storytelling.

For some fun, check out Jorge Cham's "PhD Comics" for some humor about college life. He earned a Ph.D. in robotics from Stanford University and taught at Caltech. He brings a sense of humor to education, comics, radio, and television.

Vintage comic books are wildly popular and major cities have literally dozens of comic book shops. New comic book creators can find a venue for their work in print, in social media, and on a host of other sites.

USING NEW TECHNOLOGIES TO AWE AND INSPIRE

This moment is exciting. New paradigms of drawing and painting awaken as technology expands, disrupting every facet of life. Thus, we live in a time when rapid change will require that we think differently and consider art with a new pair of glasses. The future of humanity and all other living things depends on those who can think past today, imagine tomorrow, and solve problems along the way. You live at a critical juncture where 5G, 6G, and 7G will mesh with digital currencies and Metaverse spaces. We will barely recognize our current existence by 2050. Much of that transformation will happen as a function of innovators who will invent tomorrow.

Your abilities in drawing, creating, illustrating, and storytelling will be invaluable in your life. However, the Metaverse is an amazing gateway for artists to enter, especially those with digital design skills. The Metaverse is a thrilling new arena currently in construction. Graphic artists, illustrators, animators, and storytellers will be high in demand to set up buildings, offices, and studios. Every person will have their own avatar. Someone will need to design these virtual people who will be ordered to specification. Already clothing designs in the fashion world are being generated and sold in the Metaverse. Enter to see the possibilities for you. One thing I can tell you is that if you continue in this direction and build related skills, you should have no problem finding people who need your talents.

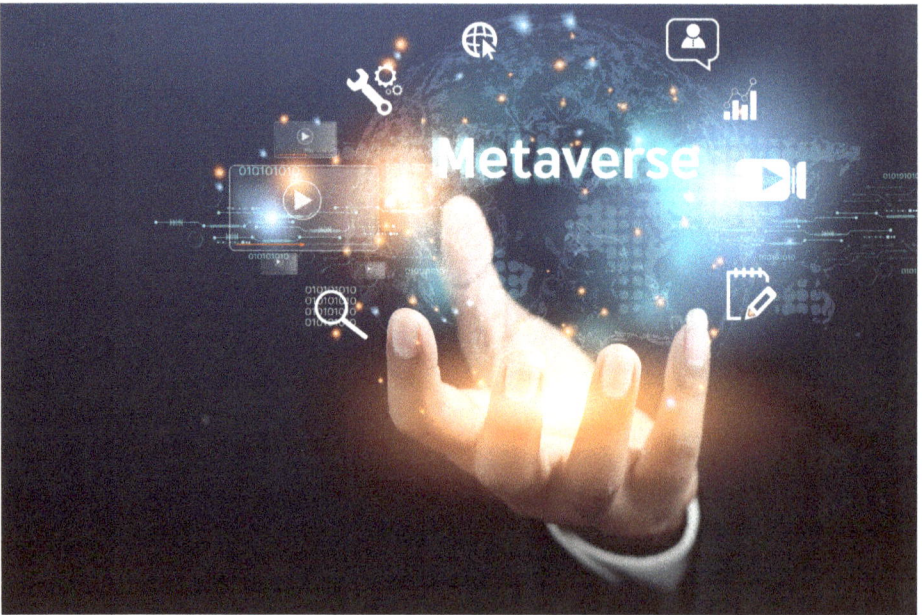

CHALLENGING CONVENTION

The definition of unique is to do something different. Uninhibited creativity is fundamental to the work. Inquisitive experimentation is integral to being an artist and blazing a trail toward your distinctive style. However, not everything you try will succeed. Some ideas will suffer the slings and arrows of those around you who question your abilities or simply cannot understand your work. You can continue unabated or try something new. Feedback is good, though it sometimes stings. Use the feedback or not.

This is your journey, not theirs. After all, this is art. It is your imagination that you are letting loose, and, in this space of vulnerability, you may feel insecure. Keep pushing through to new possibilities. You will find your lane.

HOPE AND PRAGMATISM

As an artist, Imagineer, and storyteller, you will construct the foundation for civilization's future. Begin this journey by stepping into the possibilities of today and the augmented realities of tomorrow. There are many directions you can take with your creative artistry. The combination of complex concepts will add to the challenge and intrigue of your career. The programs and colleges profiled in this book offer varied paths for you to explore. Choose the direction that makes the most sense to you. The information contained within will lead you on your way.

Every child is an artist, the problem is staying an artist when you grow up.

- Pablo Picasso

CHAPTER 2

YOUR FUTURE IN ILLUSTRATION, CARTOONING, AND COMIC BOOK DESIGN

"A growing number of contemporary American comic books are being written as literature aimed at a general readership of adults and concerned, not with the traditionally escapist themes of comics, but with issues such as the clash of cultures in American history, the burdens of guilt and suffering passed on within families, and the trials and small triumphs of the daily workaday world."

– Joseph Witek

Illustrators arouse the imagination and illuminate issues. In college, you will learn fine arts while focusing on drawing and digital skills. In each class, you will refine your talents. Your storytelling abilities will come alive. What stories do you want to tell? You create the narrative and the art by building an appreciation for illustration's history, developing skills in visual arts, constructing characters for cartooning, animation, and gaming, learning the editorial arts for newspapers and magazines, and contemplating sequential storytelling for graphic novels and children's books.

In studio spaces, creativity is unleashed. Artists, inspired to invent the future, blend vision and wonder with the nuts and bolts of the tools of their trade. Students studying illustration, cartooning, and comic book design are invited to set free the barriers of their minds-eye and visualize what has yet to be considered. Space and time, inhibiting to some, are merely a given entity in which to create. The possible career pursuits are only limited by your imagination.

All we have to decide is what to do with the time that is given us.

– J.R.R. Tolkein, *The Hobbit and Lord of the Rings*

SELLING YOUR ART

Unsurprisingly, more people are purchasing art online than in any other location. The pandemic closed many galleries. Some moved their artwork online and are seeing more sales via the Internet than in their showroom. However, there are also a wide array of online stores offering avenues to sell your art. This moment is exciting since there is a range of possibilities for your work to be shown and for you to be paid for your creative genius. Art of all kinds can be sold in these virtual shops from drawings, paintings, and illustrations to ceramics, sculptures, and crafts.

With fewer middlemen taking a cut, an artist can fluidly transition directly from canvas to screen to customer. For example, FineArtAmerica offers independent artists a venue to sell their wall art as framed or canvas prints, posters or art prints, or in collections of apparel, tapestries, or tech-centered. They boast of selling more than five million museum-quality products to buyers worldwide. It's fun just flipping through the screens of paintings, photographs, digital art, illustrations, mixed media, and originals. There is even a "Meet the Artist" center where you can post your story and your art.

ArtPal also represents more than two hundred thousand artists. Since ArtPal is a free gallery with no membership fees, buyers can browse and shop without the hassle of some of the other sites. Artists can sell their items or set the site for print on demand. Custom framing is another feature buyers appreciate. ArtPal site sells art in the following categories - paintings & prints, photography, drawings & illustrations, digital art, sculptures & carvings, ceramics & pottery, glass, jewelry, textile & apparel, crafts, and other art. Browse the site just to get inspiration. Merely reading some of the bios could be inspirational. A few are in multiple languages.

Amazon also sells art. Well, Amazon sells pretty much everything, but Amazon Art is a viable venue for 2D art. Unfortunately, 3D art is not included, but there is a location to sell crafts at Amazon Handmade. In the Amazon Art area, you can click on acrylic, oil, archival digital, watercolor, lithographs, landscape, floral, animals, architecture, nautical, and maps. You can also shop by height, width, color, or price. Since there are so many choices, use the search tool on the left side to help you sort through the thousands of offerings. Merely flipping through the digital pages will inspire you to stop what you are doing and get back to creating your art.

For those passionate about art, there are numerous other third-party websites like ArtFinder, ArtNet, ArtPlease, ArtPlode, Art Storefronts, Artsy, Azucar Gallery, Casetify, Displate, Ebay, Etsy, Minted, OnlineGallery.art, Picta Design, RedBubble, Saatchi Art, Shopify, Singulart, Society6, Storenvy, UGallery, Vsual, and Zazzle. While I do not recommend any specific site over another, this is a good place to start looking to sell your art. Of course, you have greater control by selling your work on your own website, but you need a fanbase first that you can build through friend groups, teaching, lectures, or social media. Additionally, you can also make art to order on Fiverr.

Most people enjoy expressions of art in their homes and offices. Art inspires, reflecting our deeper thoughts and the world around us. Creating, sharing, and displaying art are fun ways to live life expressively. As you plan your future, remember, there are many possible doors to enter, you just need to choose the right one for you.

FOR LOVE OR MONEY
PURSUE ART FOR YOUR DESIRE TO CREATE

If you hunger to explore art, you are in the right place. Motivational author, Marsha Sinetar, said, "Do what you love, and the money will follow." Thus, if art is your passion, you will either make your living as a professional artist, pursue art as a hobby, or translate the lessons you learn to another career or field of interest. You will learn how to use various media, for sure. However, in college, you will also learn storytelling through words and art, social media marketing, communication, presentation, and inventiveness. Each morning you will awaken with a burning desire to create or simply experiment.

The knowledge you obtain in college might also take you on a path toward education. Teaching is a noble field, offering endless inspiration. Kids, eager to experiment, use art as a form of play, diving into their paint and canvas with unbridled exuberance. Mahatma Gandhi once said, "If you want real peace in the world, start with children." Their innocence, enthusiasm, and idealism remove the bounds of learned anger and resentment. You can touch the future by empowering kids through the medium of art. You will be surprised at what they can produce when they are led on a path toward peace, possibility, and friendship.

Though you might consider teaching in a local school or college, private classes offer another option. No matter what you do with your skills, you will have opportunities to use them for the rest of your life.

MUCH TO LEARN IN COLLEGE

Studying art in college will not only teach you new techniques, but also allow you to examine, test, and collaborate with those who have similar interests. You will pursue a curriculum of classes in an artistic community encouraging you to advance your skills and inspire you to push the bounds of your creativity. Professional artists who serve as professors and have impressive credentials share their wisdom. You will learn in a unique studio environment surrounded by other extraordinarily talented individuals.

Ultimately, your portfolio will be your calling card, not your classes, professors, or colleges you choose to attend. There is no shortcut to success in this field, though learning to market yourself is essential. Diligence is required as you differentiate yourself as an artist with a distinctive style. Networking is also invaluable, supported by a talent pool of amazing students and professors who have connections. You do not need a college education to be successful, though it can open doors.

You will learn how to manage time and quickly evaluate the status of your projects while gaining valuable feedback from your peers. On group projects, collaborating can be challenging and exhilarating at the same time. Each member must listen attentively and conceptualize options while proposing ideas and creating a clear line of communication. By discussing opportunities for improvement, students can efficiently and effectively cooperate in crafting the best outcome.

The journey you are taking will have its ups and downs, but you will have stories to tell for the rest of your life. Your education may have unpredictable elements, and pitfalls may lay in your path. Since you have endured a pandemic and the repercussions of a war, you are imbued with a few doses of resilience. You will be tested in your illustration, cartooning, and comic book program as there is much to learn in a short amount of time.

You are embarking on a thrilling, demanding, and disciplined pursuit. You will work with extremely skilled and brilliant students who started creating art and crafts when they entered elementary school. Some have worked in businesses and have talents that will blow you away. Some classmates will produce professional-quality artwork. Do not let their abilities bring you down or make you feel as if you are not good enough. On the contrary, you will add your element and learn more during college. Besides, your enthusiasm will show through in your work and effort. Recognizing your potential, commitment, and attitude, people will be awed at your creations as you also step back to appreciate your work.

Enjoy the experience.

CHAPTER 3

ACADEMIC PREPARATION: ART, LIFE, AND SCHOOL FOUNDATIONS FOR FUTURE COURSEWORK

"Comic books are history. Emerging from the shifting interaction of politics, culture, audience tastes, and the economics of publishing, comic books have helped to frame a worldview and define a sense of self for the generations who have grown up with them."

– Bradford W. Wright

YOUR FUTURE IS DIRECTLY AHEAD OF YOU

The power and promise of 5G, 6G, and 7G will advance art and storytelling in revolutionary rather than evolutionary ways. Computing power, many times faster than today, will allow for quick permutations of design options and animations never before possible. Artists and other professionals will collaborate on holograms in shared spaces with members who need not be physically present.

Clearly visualized 3-D animations of illustrated designs using virtual reality will allow customers and patrons to experience what has not yet been created. Augmented reality will add to this experience by providing the viewer a user experience, possibly, one day, in the Metaverse. Stories will be told in new spaces and environments with fully automated computer design and programming tools. Group members will be able to adapt works for publication or showcase imagery in quick iterations, allowing for a near-real representation as each person analyzes the form and function within a digital gallery or pages of a text.

ACADEMIC PREPARATION

You are headed toward art mastery. To gain admission to your dream college you must be smart and talented. Even if the admission's requirements do not require a portfolio, and many do, to be successful, there are numerous preparatory skills you must develop as if you were presenting your work to a committee. Plan for your future now. Talent is only the beginning.

In high school, or college if you plan to transfer into a program, you must build solid skills in studio training inside and/or outside of school. The more exceptional artwork you can present to an admissions committee within their guidelines the better. Some mix of drawing, painting, ceramics, sculpture, 3-D design, and digital art are key components of a portfolio, though not all of these skills are necessary. Some applicants have never taken graphic design and are not penalized. Nevertheless, foundational skills in your craft and art theory are important.

COMPELLING REASONS TO STUDY ILLUSTRATION, CARTOONING, & COMIC BOOK ART

1. Freedom of creative expression
2. Mind explosion of ideas and possibilities
3. Desire to tell stories that empower, stimulate, or make people laugh
4. Love for experimentation with colors, forms, styles, shapes, and media
5. Sensory experience when witnessing captivating imagery
6. Emotional feeling that beckons you into art's space
7. The chance to turn your love into a lifetime career
8. Self-expression, self-confidence, and self-awareness
9. Individuality, unique flair, and distinctive style

IS ATTENDING COLLEGE FOR ILLUSTRATION WORTH IT?

Art has the power to relieve stress and awaken the senses. School is unempowering for those who are disenchanted with memorizing chapters of text, reading endless charters, and solving problems that seem to have no practical use. Learning math, science, and history present a one-size-fits-all model, where everyone marches in line and dutifully follows the requirements. However, there is something useful, presentable, and magical about art.

In its many forms, art enlivens. If you have practiced art, you may have a favorite medium to express yourself and define your distinct style. However, with a degree concentrated on illustration, character development, and comic book art, you will learn many additional styles and techniques.

The immersive college experience will expose you to the practices of great artists and alternative methodologies of contemporary idea generators today. You will discover a wide range of options in each art class and determine the styles and techniques you prefer. Instructors, guest lecturers, and workshop hosts will help you continue to improve your skills while offering you feedback to go to the next level.

CAN ARTISTS MAKE A LIVING?

Since money and time are valuable commodities, the question of worth, value, and future income always crop up in my college counseling sessions. Consider your future wisely before making such a big decision, though I believe that "where there is a will, there is a way." This means, of course, that you must be dedicated to your craft, have a vision for where you are headed, be persistent in taking opportunities to practice, and have the wisdom to make smart choices.

In a world where social media can connect you to customers, you can show your art through many different sites without leaving your studio, which may be your apartment. You may choose to be an intrepid frontrunner by creating a gallery in the Metaverse and selling your artwork using NFTs, bitcoin, or another digital payment system.

Amazing college professors who are successful in their own right will suggest ways to sell your art and may even link you to their contacts. In the process, you will discover your brand of professionalism along with a calling card of images that allow others to understand what you offer.

"THERE IS NO ROYAL ROAD TO GEOMETRY" - EUCLID

When a student asked Euclid if there was an easier way to learn geometry, he cautioned that discipline and persistence are essential. Hard work is absolutely necessary. Additionally, there is no one way to succeed, just as there is no one way to paint. You may choose to draw images for a company, sell your artwork, teach others fine arts, or support other artists by sharing your wisdom. Either way, art is a versatile skill. Other professional options include arts management, museum studies, television, entertainment, fashion, education, art therapy, and much more.

You could manage an art store or create your own online webstore. You might find that critiquing art is of interest or helping other people market their art empowering. Museums have a variety of positions that require the knowledge of trained artists.

Teaching is often considered a fallback. Yet, many are inspired by the innocence and dreams of young artists. Finally, art therapy has excellent potential to make a difference in someone's life. So many people were demoralized by the pandemic and could not find their way forward toward hope and possibility. You could support others to find their peace of mind. My point is that, as you develop your skills, your talent is not wasted, not lost, not valueless. You can be a source of empowerment and strength for others.

ARTS MANAGEMENT

This field has grown in the past decade as more people seek ways to contemplate life through art. The job of an arts manager is to know and understand art while also having a business sense to manage a private or public art institution. Thus, arts managers efficiently run the business and share the creative inspirations of artists, performers, or designers. With skills in planning events, managing talent, envisioning space, communicating messages, and hosting guests, you will serve society in significant ways. For example, suppose you want to inspire both artists and patrons alike, giving artists the freedom to express themselves while offering visitors or purchasers the chance to learn, identify, feel, and imagine. In that case, arts management is an excellent profession, and it can pay well.

ARTS/ENTERTAINMENT AGENT

This profession is perfect for the person who is inspired to help artists find locations to promote, show, and sell their artwork. Many times, artists consume themselves in their art. They immerse themselves in the vision and technical precision of their craft. However, they are not skilled in public relations, advertising, promotion, website development, social media, and the legal aspects of contracts, releases, and intellectual property. Many artists want to focus on their craft rather than pounding the pavement to find shows, exhibitions, events, venues, and other opportunities. Here, an agent may be invaluable. An arts/entertainment agent ensures that excellent art of all kinds has a platform to be seen. Imagine for a moment how many thousands of extraordinarily talented artists exist whose work is never seen except possibly among a small enclave of other talented artists or friends. Thus, those who are 'successful' are 'discovered' or promoted. They are not always the best artists. You might find representing talented people uplifting. Otherwise, you might contract with an arts/entertainment agent yourself.

FASHION DESIGN, TEXTILE DESIGN, AND MERCHANDISING

Illustrators with an eye for color, style, and design often express this through their own hair, clothing, or accessories. Often, they enjoy pondering other individuals' attires as models of fashion or ways to augment their look. Starting with envisioning and sketching fabric designs before they are woven, or designing them after the cloth is created, there is an immense amount of artistry involved with clothing creation. Attending fashion shows, buying next season's designs, marketing outfits, and displaying items in stores takes the flair of a creative mind. Individuals with these interests may discover that segments of the fashion industry are immensely appealing.

TEACHING, EDUCATION, AND TRAINING

Kids clamor to create. Their imaginations run wild with ideas. Self-expression and introspection inspire the exploration of innovative art. People young and old relay ideas onto paper, a computer, or media like photography or film. Some perform in voice, dance, and acting. As a result, there are numerous jobs in private and public education. Schools everywhere hire art teachers. Families hire art coaches. Private studios conduct workshops and training. Furthermore, college art professors can make $100,000/year teaching students while continuing to practice their craft.

In the United States, in 2021, there were approximately 130,000 public and private K-12 schools, according to the National Center for Educational Statistics. Furthermore, during the 2019-2020 school year, there were 3,982 degree-granting higher education colleges and universities – 2,679 4-year and 1,303 2-year institutions.[1] In California alone, during the 2020-2021 school year, there were 10,545 K-12 public schools and another 1,296 charter schools.[2] Thus, there are numerous schools in which you may choose to work.

ART THERAPY

Art therapists are clinicians who support people of all ages as mental health practitioners. They provide services and counseling through the active practice of art-making and other creative processes. Art can be a healing power, allowing individuals to improve their physical and mental abilities while reducing both stress and conflict and improving both self-esteem and self-awareness. Using applied psychology, art therapists improve the human experience in a psychotherapeutic relationship. Art therapists must be credentialed and certified to practice in hospitals, schools, veteran's clinics, private practice, rehabilitation centers, psychiatric facilities, community clinics, crisis centers, forensic institutions, and senior communities.

To become an art therapist, you must attend graduate school and earn a master's or doctoral degree. However, there are undergraduate programs in art therapy that can get you on your way. A Master of Arts in Art Therapy can also lead

---

1   NCES, "Digest of Education Statistics," U.S. Department of Education, 2020 Tables and Figures, https://nces.ed.gov/programs/digest/d20/tables/dt20_317.10.asp

2   California Department of Education, "Fingertip Facts on Education in California", 2020-2021, https://www.cde.ca.gov/ds/ad/ceffingertipfacts.asp

to a Master of Arts in Marriage and Family Studies or a Ph.D. in Art Therapy. Most graduate programs prepare graduates to sit for the Art Therapy Registration (ATR), Creative Arts Therapist (LCAT), and Licensed Professional Clinical Counselor (LPCC).

UNDERGRADUATE ART THERAPY PROGRAMS
AMERICAN ART THERAPY ASSOCIATION

Anna Maria College (MA)

Capital University (OH)

Converse College (SC)

Edgewood College (WI)

Long Island University, Post Campus (NY)

Mars Hill University (NC)

Mercyhurst University (PA)

Millikin University (IL)

Mount Mary University (WI)

Notre Dame of Maryland University (MD)

Russell Sage College (NY)

Seton Hill University (PA)

St. Thomas Aquinas College (NY)

Temple University (PA)

University of the Arts (PA)

University of Tampa (FL)

Ursuline College (OH)

CAAHEP ACCREDITED GRADUATE ART THERAPY PROGRAMS[3]

Adler Graduate School (MN)

Albertus Magnus College (CT)

Antioch University Seattle (WA)

Caldwell University (NJ)

Drexel University (PA)

Eastern Virginia Medical School (VA)

Edinboro University (PA)

Emporia State University (KS)

Florida State University (FL)

George Washington University (DC)

Hofstra University (NY)

Indiana Univ.-Purdue Univ.-IUPUI (IN)

Lewis & Clark College (OR)

Long Island University – Post (NY)

Loyola Marymount University (CA)

Maywood University (PA)

Naropa University (CO)

Nazareth College (NY)

New York University (NY)

Southern Illinois University (IL)

Southwestern College (NM)

Springfield College (MA)

St. Mary-of-the-Woods College (IN)

University of Louisville (KY)

Ursuline College (OH)

---

3   CAAHEP, "Commission on Accreditation" https://www.caahep.org/Students/Find-a-Program.aspx

LIMITLESS POSSIBILITIES

The preparation you receive will not restrict you. One of my students went from painting to game design, which required a year of focused digital skills, but he now has an amazing job that he enjoys. Drawing and illustration are fundamental to any area of art. Your options will be completely open, providing you with the freedom to choose.

The scope of art is expanding with new frontiers that offer opportunities never before imaginable. For example, new industries and manufacturing facilities need artists to imagine and invent advertising, products, tools, toys, fashions, graphics, and imagery on websites and soon the Metaverse. The ever-expanding need is why some colleges like Savannah College of Art and Design, Maryland Institute College of Art (MICA), and Ringling College of Art and Design have a dozen or more specialized majors in art, giving students the flexibility to adapt their program with new areas of interest.

Studying art will also keep you creative, allowing you to explore your evolving artistic style. Art is increasingly recognized as a valuable skill. If you are passionate about this pursuit, one day, your efforts will bear fruit!

CHAPTER 4

ART, DESIGN, AND LIFE EXPERIENCES: INTERNSHIPS AND PROGRAMS FOR HIGH SCHOOL AND COLLEGE STUDENTS

"The principle of true art is not to portray, but to evoke."

– Jerzy Kosinski

S tart early to gain drawing, design, photography, and film experiences. Internships and summer programs are as important in your educational pathway as coursework. The lessons you learn from working collaboratively and collegially with other art and design-focused mentors may be different but equally important. Historian and scholar, W.E.B. DuBois (1868-1963), a founding member of the NAACP and the first Black American to earn a Ph.D. at Harvard said, "Education must not simply teach work - it must teach life." Your college, experiential, and life education go hand-in-hand, driven by purpose and foresight since life truly is a journey, not a destination.

Note: This list is not exhaustive, and it is not an endorsement of any program. Dates, program description, and program length may be changed from year to year.

SUMMER CAMPS & PROGRAMS FOR ART, DESIGN, FILM, PHOTOGRAPHY, AND ARCHITECTURE

Alabama

Auburn University – Architecture Camp – Creative Writing – Industrial Design

One week – Three Session Options – Full Scholarships Available (apply by April 1)
Students produce designs working directly with professors.
Camp counselors support students with 24/7 questions, safety, and supervision.

Tuskegee University Taylor School of Architecture & Construction Science

Virtual Preview of Architecture and Construction at Tuskegee (V-PACT) 3-hour Virtual Program

Preview Architecture & Construction Science 2-Week Program

Arizona

Arcosanti – Re-Imagined Urbanism – 6-week discussion-based classes - AZ

Combining architecture and ecology (arcology), you can learn in the World's First Prototype Arcology.

Core values: (1) Frugality and Resourcefulness, (2) Ecological Accountability, (3) Experiential Learning, and (4) Leaving a Limited Footprint, Arcosanti is juxtaposed to mass consumerism, urban sprawl, unchecked consumption, and social isolation.

Arkansas

University of Arkansas – In Person & Virtual Design Camp – Fayetteville, AK

In-Person Grades 9-12 - design projects, studio groups, tours, & meetings with local designers.

No fee; completely remote; design camp lessons embedded; students are paired with a faculty member in a studio group.

Advanced Design Camp: students entering Grades 11-12, 2 weeks in Fayetteville

California

Academy of Art Institute – San Francisco

4-6 weeks – Advertising, Animation/VFX, Architecture, Fashion, Fine Art, Game Development, Graphic Design

Illustration, Industrial Design, Motion Pictures, Music Production, Photography, Writing for Film, TV, & Digital Media

Laguna College of Art & Design Pre-College Program – Laguna Beach, CA

Animation, Sculpture, Drawing Fundamentals, Figure Drawing, Graphic Design

School of Creative & Performing Arts (SOCAPA) – Occidental College (13-18-year-olds)

2-week, 3-week - learn Filmmaking, Screenwriting, Dance, Music, Photography

SCI-Arc (Southern California Institute of Architecture) Immersive 4-week Summer Program (Design Immersion Days) – Los Angeles

Introduction to the academic and professional world of architecture – Grades 9-12

Stanford University – 8-Week Summer Courses and 3-Week Arts Institute

Architecture, Art, Drawing, Dance, Creative Writing, Music, and Photography

UCLA Summer Jumpstart Summer Art Inst, Digital Media Arts Inst., Digital Filmmaking Inst., Game Lab Inst.

2-week program - Portfolio development– credit available

Drawing, Painting, Photography, Sculpture, Video Art, Animation, and Game Design

USC Summer Film, Writing, and Architecture Programs – Los Angeles

2-4-week program, "Creative Writing Workshop", "Comedy Performance", "Exploration into Architecture"

Connecticut

Summer Studio: Discovering Graphic Design (AIGA) – Bridgeport, CT

Free 4-week hands-on program for Bridgeport rising juniors and seniors

Week 1 – Music Festival Poster, Week 2 – Digital Media Poster

Week 3 – Animating Your Ideas, Week 4 – Portfolio Art for College Applications

District of Columbia

Catholic University School of Architecture and Planning

Summer High School Program - 2-week Residential (Two Session Options)

George Washington University Digital Storytelling Pre-College Program – July

Produce stories with smartphones, learn storyboarding, and broadcast through social media

Craft ideas, capture images, & create compelling content, including character development

Georgetown University – 1-week – Creative Writing – Publishing

Fiction, Short Story, Poetry, and Professional Writing; visit literary hubs

Florida

Florida Atlantic University – Boca Raton, FL and Ft. Lauderdale, FL

School of Architecture – July (Three Session Options)

July 3-week program for rising sophomores, juniors, seniors, and students in their first 2 years of college

Certificate of Completion Awarded – Enrollment on a first-come, first-served basis

Portfolio development, fabrication, architectural education, portfolio display, critique

University of Florida Design Exploration Program (DEP)

3-week Residential Immersion into the architectural studio environment.

Construction of studio design projects, teamwork, seminars, field trips, architectural theory.

University of Miami Summer Scholars, Explorations in Architecture & Design – Coral Gables, FL

3-week Residential program; 6 college credits; Design, Graphics, and Theory.

Architecture, Landscape Architecture, Historic Preservation; Urban Planning.

Studio experience with drawing, model making, drafting, CAD, visual analysis.

Georgia

Emory University – Atlanta, GA – 2-, 4-, 6-Week Writing Programs

Journalism, Dramatic Writing, Media & Politics, Psychology & Fiction

Georgia Institute of Technology Pre-College Design Program – Atlanta, GA

2-week Residential program – College of Design – Grades 11 & 12 (Two Session Options)

Architecture, Building Construction, Industrial Design, and Music Technology

Savannah College of Art & Design – Savannah, GA

2-week College of Design Residential program –– Grades 11 & 12 - Courses include Advertising, Animation, Virtual Reality, Illustration, Storyboarding, Photography, Painting, Fashion, Digital Film, Graphic Design, and Industrial Design

Illinois

Illinois Institute of Technology Summer Introduction to Architecture

2-week Experiment in Architecture for HS students – Comprehensive overview

1-week Exploration in Architecture for middle school students – studio-based, firm visits, field trips, projects.

Northwestern University – National HS Institute

5-week Film & Video, Music, Speech & Debate, Theatre

School of the Art Institute of Chicago – Early College Program for HS Students

1-, 2-, 4-week Residential programs in Painting, Drawing, Animation, Comics/Graphic Novels, and Fashion Design.

Portfolio development programs; earn college credit. Full-tuition scholarships are available.

Southern Illinois University Carbondale – Kid Architecture

1-week Elementary Grades, Middle School & High School Architecture Camp

University of Illinois at Chicago Architecture - HiArch Summer High School Program

1-, 2-week (July) - HS students are introduced to the culture of architecture, design, thinking, and making.

University of Chicago Creative Writing Immersion

"Collegiate Writing: Awakening Into Consciousness" and "Creative Writing: Fiction"

Indiana

University of Notre Dame Summer Scholars Program

2-weeks HS Students – Film, Photography, Performing Arts - studios, seminars, and field trips

Iowa

Iowa State University – College of Design - HS Design Camps

1-week HS Students – Architecture, Studio/Fine Arts, Graphic Design, Interior Design, & Industrial Design

Maryland

Maryland Institute College of Art (MICA) – Baltimore, MD

2-, 3-, 5-week HS Students – Live instruction, studio time, workshops, artist talks, collaboration, feedback, critique, evaluation

Massachusetts

Boston College - Boston, MA – Creative Writing Seminar Program

3-week (July) Residential Program – HS Students – nonfiction, fiction, poetry – hone techniques

Create & edit the class literary journal and present writings at a public reading

Harvard University GSD Design Discovery – Cambridge, MA (Ages 18-mid-career professionals)

3-week Residential Program – Architecture, Landscape, Urban Planning & Design

Physical modeling, fabrication, assembly

Harvard Summer Program for High School Students

2-week non-credit program; 7-week college credit program (live in campus dorms)

Credit classes include: Creating Comics & Graphic Novels; Drawing & the Digital Age; Advertising, Landscape, & Visual Imagery; Creative Writing

Massachusetts College of Art & Design – 4-Week Art Immersion Program

Students take 3 foundation courses; closing exhibition

Massachusetts Institute of Technology – Urbaneframe – Cambridge, MA

HS Students - Summer Design-Build Project

CAD, drafting, sketching, mapping and context study, historical research, carpentry & construction

Tufts University – 6-Week Writing Intensive

Writing exercises, evaluation from professors, revise, develop papers that build on a theme

Savannah College of Art & Design – Savannah, GA - SCAD 5-week Rising Star Program

Week-long Summer Seminars & 2-week College of Design Residential program

Courses include Advertising, Animation, Virtual Reality, Illustration, Storyboarding,

Photography, Painting, Fashion, Digital Film, Graphic Design, and Industrial Design

University of Massachusetts Amherst Pre-College – Amherst, MA

1-, 2-, 3-week Residential Intensives Grades 10-12

3-D Design, 3-D Animation, Building & Construction Technology; Combatting the Climate Crisis

Summer Engineering Institute, Summer Design Academy, Programming for Aspiring Scientists

Wellesley College – Wellesley, MA

2-week Residential Program - EXPLO Pre-College + Career for Grades 10-12

Three session options; Topics include – AI, Entrepreneurship, Engineering, Medicine, Law, CSI

Youth Design Boston (AIGA) – Boston, MA

Summer Graphic Design Internship & Mentoring Program

Michigan

Andrews University School of Architecture & Interior Design - Renaissance Kids – Berrien Springs, MI

Virtual Studio Projects; lecture; community build projects

Interlochen Center for the Arts – Summer Arts Camp – 1-6 Weeks

Creative Writing, Dance, Art, Motion Picture, Music, Theatre, Visual Arts

University of Michigan – Stamps School of Art & Design – BFA Preview

3-week (June/July)– HS Students – Creative retreat with state-of-the-art facilities & museum excursions

Missouri

Washington University in St. Louis – Creative Writing Institute and HS Summer Scholars Program

2-week program – fiction, nonfiction, and poetry; morning writer's workshops – editing and sharing work

5-8 week – Dance, Journalism, Photography, Music, Drama, Photojournalism

University of Missouri Kansas City – Department of Architecture, Urban Planning & Design MA

Design Discovery Program – Architecture, Interior Design, Landscape Architecture

3-day (July) Non-Residential Program – HS Students/Current College Students

Nebraska

University of Nebraska College of Architecture – Lincoln, NE

6-day (June) Residential Program – Grades 11 & 12 – Studio training; architectural design; scholarships

New Jersey

New Jersey Institute of Technology – Hillier College of Architecture & Design

1-week (July) Residential Program – HS Students – Architecture, Interior Design, Industrial Design, Digital Design

Summer Architecture + Design Programs (2 Start Dates)

New York

AIA New York – Center for Architecture

1-week (July) Residential Program – HS Students – Architecture

Programs for Grades 3-12 include Architectural Design Studio, Drawing Architecture, Rooftop Dwelling, Dream House, Treehouses, Skyscrapers, Green Island Home, Subway Architecture, Waterfront City, Parks & Playground Design, and Neighborhood Design

Columbia University - New York, NY – Summer Immersion

3-week July-August Residential Program – Architecture, Creative Writing, Drawing, Filmmaking, Photography, Theater, or Visual Arts

Cooper Union - New York, NY – Summer Art Intensive

4-week July-August Residential Programs – Portfolio Development, Exhibition, Anthology Publication

Animation, Creative Writing, Photography, Drawing, Graphic Design, & Stop Animation

Cornell University – Ithaca, NY – Precollege Studies and 3-Week Transmedia: Image, Sound, Motion Program

3-, 6-, 9-week June-August Residential Program; Drawing and New Media

(collage, drawing, digital photography, screen printing, & video)

Architecture: Design Studio, Culture, and Society, Architectural Science & Technology

New York University Summer Art Intensive

4-week Immersive program in Digital & Video, Sculpture, or Visual Arts

Parsons School of Design – New York and Paris

4-week - Online and on-campus summer programs for students from 3rd grade to 12th

NYC - Portfolio building in 3-credit immersive Design, Studio Art, Photography, Illustration, Game Design

Paris Program – Design & Mgmt, Explorations in Drawing & Painting, Fashion Design

Rensselaer Polytechnic University – Troy, NY

Architecture Career Discovery Program

School of Creative & Performing Arts (SOCAPA) – New York (13-18-year-olds)

2-, 3-week - Learn Filmmaking, Screenwriting, Dance, Music, Photography

Sotheby's Summer Institute – Pre-College, Undergrad, Graduate, and Professional

New York, London, and Virtual Programs

Intensives in Painting & Drawing, Curating, Luxury Marketing, Art Crime/Art Law, Fashion, and Art Business

Syracuse University – Syracuse, NY – On-Campus and Online Programs for HS Students

2-, 3-, 6-week programs 3-D Studio Art; Sculpture; Architecture; Design Studies; Writing Immersion

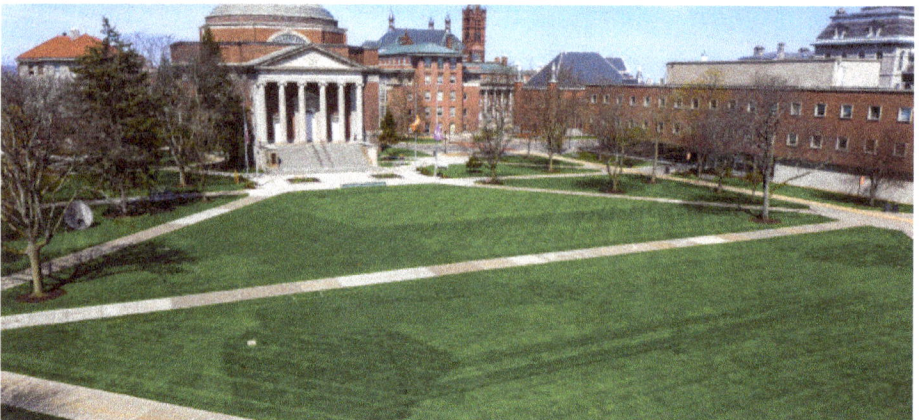

Oklahoma

University of Oklahoma Architecture Summer Academy

1-week (June) Residential Program – HS Students – Architecture, Interior Design, Construction Science

Design in Action: Creativity, Innovation, and Sustainability Shaping the Built Environment

Pennsylvania

Carnegie Mellon University Pre-College Art Program - Pittsburgh, PA

3-, 4-, 6-week (July-August) Residential Program – Intensive Studio Studies

Portfolio development in Drawing, Sculpture, Animation, and Concept Studio Art

Chestnut Hill College Global Solutions Lab

Interactive Global Simulation, Electrifying Africa, & UN Sustainable Development Goals

1-week programs – HS Students – Intensive collaborative team solutions to big problems

Drexel University Westphal College of Media Arts & Design – Discovering Architecture

2-week Residential Program – HS Students – Intensive Studio Architecture Program

Visit prominent architectural, multi-disciplinary design offices; meet architects

Maywood University Pre-College Summer Workshop School of Architecture

2-week (July) Residential Program – HS Students – Design Your Future Architecture Program

Pennsylvania State University Architecture & Landscape Architecture Summer Camp

1-week (July) – HS Students –Architecture, Graphics, Design, and the Built Environment Program

Temple University Tyler School of Art and Architecture Pre-College Architecture Program

Architecture Institute – Philadelphia, PA

2-week (July-August) Residential Program – HS Students – Studio Architecture

Rhode Island

Brown University – 1-4 Weeks – Art Themed Courses

Creative Writing, Music, Studio Art, Art History

Rhode Island School of Design Pre-College School of Design – Providence, RI

6-week (June-July) Residential Program – HS Students – Foundational Art & Design Studies

Figure drawing, projects, trips, exhibitions

Roger Williams University High School Summer Academy in Architecture

4-week (July-August) Residential Program – Grades 11 & 12 – Explore Studio Architecture

Seminars, fieldwork, studio, portfolio development

South Carolina

Clemson University Pre-College School of Architecture Program

1-week (July-August) Residential Program – Grades 7-12

Engineering Design, Mechanical Engineering, Civil Engineering, Intelligent Vehicles, Materials Engineering

Tennessee

The University of Memphis Discovering Architecture + Design

1-day – HS Students – Design programs on architecture, interior design, and the built environment

The University of Tennessee, Knoxville College of Architecture + Design

1-week UT Summer Design Camp (July) Residential – HS Students

Immersive architecture, graphic design, and professional practice program

Vanderbilt Summer Academy – Nashville, TN – 3-Week Program

"Digital Storytelling", "Writing Fantasy Fiction", "Math & Music", "Writing Short Stories"

Texas

Texas Tech Anson L Clark Scholars Program – Research Area: Advertising, Architecture, Art, Dance, or Theatre

7-week – Grades 11 & 12 – Residential Program (must be 17 years old by start date) – no program fee

Intensive research-based program; $500 meal card; $750 tax-free stipend

University of Houston & Wonderworks Pre-College Summer Discovery Program

Hines College of Architecture & Design – Introduction to Architecture

6-week – HS Students – Design programs with hands-on studio, field trips, and portfolio workshop

The University of Texas at Austin Summer Design Camps – 2-D Game Design, 3-D Game Design, 3-D Animation/Motion

School of Design and Creative Technologies

1-week – HS Students – portfolio development and design

Vermont

School of Creative & Performing Arts (SOCAPA) – Burlington, VT (13-18-year-olds)

2-week, 3-week - learn Filmmaking, Screenwriting, Dance, Music, Photography

Virginia

Virginia Tech Inside Architecture + Design

1-week – HS Students – Hands-on design studio architecture program

Washington

DigiPen Academy – K-12 Animation, Film, Music, Game Design Summer Programs – Redmond, WA

1-week and 2-week programs, including Teen Art & Animation; Film Scoring

Music & Sound Design; Video Game Development; Animation Masterclass

Wisconsin

The University of Wisconsin Milwaukee School of Architecture & Urban Planning

1-week – HS Students – Design program on architecture, interior design, and the built environment

CHAPTER 5

UNIVERSITY OPTIONS: EXCELLENT COLLEGE PROGRAMS FOR ILLUSTRATION & COMIC ART

"Every artist was first an amateur."

– Ralph Waldo Emerson

I n the United States, about 50 colleges offer a bachelor's degree specifically in illustration. Another 15-20 offer a master's degree in illustration. In 2021, these colleges awarded nearly 2,500 undergraduate and graduate degrees specifically in illustration. Also, approximately 300 colleges offer a 4-year accredited degree in fine art. Altogether, more than two million people in the United States have degrees in visual and performing arts, with about half specifically in visual arts. However, only about ten percent make the bulk of their income through art.

U.S. College Students – approximately 19.6 million

14.5 million attending public colleges

5.14 million attending private colleges

2,679 4-year colleges; 1,303 2-year colleges

Another interesting statistic is that undergraduate enrollment dropped more than 4% from fall 2019 to fall 2020 and another 3.5% from fall 2020 to fall 2021, representing approximately a 1,500,000 loss of students during the pandemic. However, with test-optional admissions opening the door to more students without test scores or who test poorly, more students applied to the top schools.

TOP UNDERGRADUATE SCHOOLS IN ILLUSTRATION

1. Rhode Island School of Design
2. Syracuse University
3. ArtCenter College of Design
4. Fashion Institute of Technology
5. College of Creative Studies
6. Pratt Institute
7. Rochester Inst. of Tech.
8. Maryland Institute College of Art
9. Brigham Young University
10. Virginia Commonwealth University

TOP 50 UNDERGRADUATE AND GRADUATE SCHOOLS IN ILLUSTRATION (ACCORDING TO ANIMATION CAREER REVIEW)

1. School of Visual Arts
2. ArtCenter College of Design
3. Rhode Island School of Design
4. Ringling College of Art & Design
5. Savannah College of Art & Design
6. Pratt Institute
7. Maryland Institute College of Art
8. California College of the Arts
9. Parsons School of Design
10. Otis College of Art & Design
11. Fashion Institute of Technology
12. Minneapolis College of Art & Design
13. Massachusetts College of Art & Design
14. Columbus College of Art & Design
15. College for Creative Studies
16. Kansas City Art Institute
17. Virginia Commonwealth
18. Syracuse University
19. San Jose State University
20. Cleveland Institute of Art
21. Laguna College of Art & Design
22. California State University, Fullerton
23. Washington University in St. Louis
24. Academy of Art University
25. Brigham Young University
26. California State University, Long Beach
27. Pacific Northwest College of Art
28. Milwaukee Institute of Art & Design
29. University of Central Florida
30. California State University, Northridge
31. Rocky Mountain College of Art & Design
32. University of the Arts
33. Columbia College Chicago
34. Ferris State University
35. Rochester Inst. of Tech.
36. Indiana University – Purdue
37. University of Georgia
38. Texas State University, San Marcos
39. University of Colorado, Denver
40. University of North Carolina, Charlotte
41. University of Connecticut
42. University of Arizona
43. East Carolina University
44. Belmont University
45. University of Illinois at Chicago
46. UPenn + Pennsylvania Academy of Fine Arts
47. University of Miami
48. Maine College of Art
49. Art Academy of Cincinnati
50. University of Hartford

COLLEGES GRANTING UNDERGRADUATE DEGREES IN COMIC BOOK ART

Alberta University of the Arts

Columbus College of Art & Design

Lesley Art + Design

Otis College of Art & Design

Parsons School of Design

Ringling College of Art & Design

School of the Art Institute of Chicago

School of Visual Arts

COLLEGES GRANTING GRADUATE DEGREES IN COMIC BOOK ART

California College of the Arts

Minneapolis College of Art & Design

School of Visual Arts

TOP SIXTEEN PAINTING PROGRAMS

1. Yale University
2. Rhode Island School of Design
3. School of the Art Institute of Chicago
4. Columbia University
5. Bard College
6. Boston University
7. Maryland Institute College of Art
8. UCLA
9. California Institute of the Arts
10. Hunter College - CUNY
11. Pratt Institute
12. School of Visual Arts
13. Virginia Commonwealth University
14. Cranbrook Academy of Art
15. Temple University
16. Rutgers University

COLLEGES OFFERING THE MOST BACHELOR'S DEGREES IN FINE ART EACH YEAR

1. School of the Art Institute of Chicago
2. California State University, Fullerton
3. California State University, Long Beach
4. University of North Texas
5. City University of New York
6. Florida State University
7. University of Central Florida
8. San Jose State University
9. Indiana University – Purdue
10. Hunter College - CUNY

U.S. – ACCREDITED COLLEGES FOCUSED ON ART

United States

Art Academy of Cincinnati (OH)

ArtCenter College of Design (CA)

Art Institute of Boston (MA)

Art Institute of Pittsburgh (PA)

California College of the Arts (CA)

California Institute of the Arts (CA)

Cleveland Institute of Art (OH)

College for Creative Studies (MI)

Columbia College Chicago (IL)

Cooper Union (NY)

Corcoran Col. of Art & Design - GWU (DC)

Cornish College of the Arts (WA)

Fashion Institute of Technology (NY)

Kansas City Art Institute (MO)

Kendall College of Art & Design (MI)

Laguna College of Art & Design (CA)

Lyme Academy College of Fine Arts (CT)

Maine College of Art (ME)

Maryland Institute College of Art (MD)

Mass. College of Art & Design (MA)

Memphis College of Art (TN)

Milwaukee Institute of Art & Design (WI)

Minneapolis College of Art & Design (MN)

Montserrat College of Art (MA)

Moore College of Art & Design (PA)

New Hampshire Institute of Art (NH)

N. Mich. Univ. School of Art & Design (MI)

Oregon College of Art & Craft (OR)

Otis College of Art & Design (CA)

Pacific Northwest College of Art (OR)

Parsons School of Design (NY)

Pratt Institute (NY)

Rhode Island School of Design (RI)

Ringling College of Art & Design (FL)

San Francisco Art Institute (CA)

Savannah College of Art & Design (GA)

School of the Art Institute of Chicago (IL)

School of the Museum of Fine Arts (MA)

Vermont College of Fine Arts (VT)

Watkins College of Art, Design, & Film (TN)

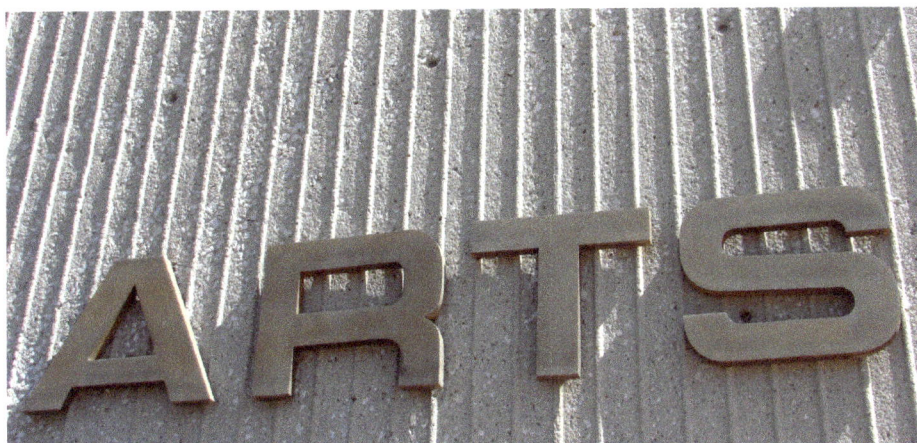

You might even want to study illustration or comic art abroad. Though international programs are not profiled in this book, some of the best are included in the following lists.

U.S. – ACCREDITED COLLEGES FOCUSED ON ART

International

Adelaide Central School of Art (Australia)

Alberta University of the Arts (Canada)

Bauhaus University Weimar (Germany)

Camberwell College of Arts (England)

Emily Carr Univ. of Art & Design (Canada)

Government College of Art & Craft (India)

Grekov Odessa Art School (Ukraine)

National Art School (Australia)

Nova Scotia College of Art & Design Univ. (Canada)

Ontario College of Art & Design Univ. (Canada)

Paris College of Art (France)

You might even want to study fine art abroad. Though international programs are not profiled in this book, some of the best are included in the following list.

2021 QS RANKED TOP UNIVERSITIES FOR ART AND DESIGN WORLDWIDE

1. Royal College of Art (U.K.)
2. University of the Arts London (U.K.)
3. Parsons School of Design (NY-USA)
4. Rhode Island School of Design (RI-USA)
5. Massachusetts Institute of Technology (MA-USA)
6. Politecnico de Milano (Italy)
7. Aalto University (Finland)
8. School of the Art Institute of Chicago (IL-USA)
9. Glasgow School of Art (U.K.)
10. Pratt Institute (NY-USA)
11. ArtCenter (CA-USA)
12. Delft University of Technology (Netherlands)
13. Design Academy Eindhoven (Netherlands)
14. Tongji University (China)
15. Goldsmiths, University of London (U.K.)
16. Royal Melbourne Institute of Technology (Australia)
17. California Institute of the Arts (CA-USA)
18. Carnegie Mellon University (PA-USA)
19. Stanford University (CA-USA)
20. Hong Kong Polytechnic University (H.K. SAR)

THE MANY ROADS TO ARTISTIC SUCCESS

There are numerous ways you can be successful in illustration and comic book design. The training you get in college can be immensely valuable, particularly while being surrounded by highly skilled practitioners in the art. There is no one road to get to your goal, just as there is not only one goal you may want to achieve. Skills in illustration offer numerous pathways and byways. Some famous artists attended smaller programs where they gained a broader or more extensive liberal arts education. Others never went to college at all. Exposure to the many different forms of art with students who have diverse interests cannot be understated.

Whichever road you take, enjoy the journey.

YEAH!!

BE DIFFERENT

CHAPTER 6

WHAT IS THE DIFFERENCE BETWEEN AN AA, AS, BA, BS, BFA, AND MFA?

"I was a painter and illustrator, so when I came to comic books, they thought I fell from the sky. They had no idea, who was this guy, how can he do all this stuff."

– Neal Adams

UNDERGRADUATE AND GRADUATE DEGREES

AA – Associate of Arts – 2-year degree

AS – Associate of Science – 2-year degree

BA – Bachelor of Arts – 4-year degree

BS – Bachelor of Science – 4-year degree

BFA – Bachelor of Fine Arts – 4-year degree with most classes focused on art

MFA – Master of Fine Arts – 1-2-year degree earned after the BA, BS, or BFA

Basically, BA and BS degrees are degrees that typically offer a liberal arts foundation along with a major or concentration in a specific subject. Meanwhile, a BFA is considered a professional arts-focused degree with fewer courses in English, science, math, social science, and the humanities. Thus, the BFA is a specialist qualification in the arts. A BA or BS degree in fine arts, illustration, graphic design, film, and animation are also valuable. The BFA is more focused on the specific area of art you choose.

The BA and BS degrees include significantly more liberal arts classes and thus are more general degrees. However, the intention of the BFA degree is for students to pursue an arts-focused curriculum, and thus there are fewer general subject courses.

Finally, while many AA or AS degrees are focused on providing technical or professional skills for art, design, film, or photography, an AA or AS in these areas are often interchangeable. Similarly, a BA or BS in illustration, comic art, and graphic design are often interchangeable. Similarly, a BA or BS in theatre-oriented degrees are often interchangeable. However, a BFA may be seen as different since there is typically more coursework focused on your specific pursuit, and thus, you may have more technical experiences and knowledge than someone who has a BA or BS.

AA – ASSOCIATE OF ARTS

The Associate of Arts degree is typically a 2-year general studies degree offered online or in-person by a community college. However, some universities offer AA degrees as well. Often, the Associate of Arts degree focused on the liberal arts has no barrier to entry, meaning that students can enter most AA programs with a high school diploma or the equivalent.

Some students take a longer or shorter time to complete the AA based upon their skills upon entering the program, certainty about the direction they are heading, and the transfer requirements for the program they desire. For example, students majoring in business may have additional business, communication, accounting, and economics requirements and need to create an academic plan early in their program to finish in two years.

AS – ASSOCIATE OF SCIENCE

The Associate of Science degree is very similar to the AA. However, the AS degree frequently emphasizes science and math and often has additional requirements.

BA – BACHELOR OF ARTS

The Bachelor of Arts degree is typically a 4-year degree offered online or in-person by a college or university. However, a few community colleges offer BA degrees as well. Some students complete their BA in fewer years depending upon AP/IB credit, dual enrollment in high school, and summer/intersession classes. College programs have stricter or less stringent requirements depending upon the school. The Bachelor of Arts degree frequently requires students to take lower-division (first and second year) liberal arts courses before taking specialized courses focused around a major or concentration in their third and fourth years.

The time required to earn a BA depends upon each student's skills and advanced placement credit when entering the program. Some students change the direction they are heading and their chosen major which can add more time. According to the , college advisors aid students in finishing "on time" though less than half of all students in the United States who start a BA program do not finish their degree in four years.[1]

BS – BACHELOR OF SCIENCE

The Bachelor of Science degree is very similar to the BA. However, the BS degree frequently emphasizes science and math and often has additional requirements.[2]

---

1   IEC NCES, "Digest of Education Statistics, Table 326.10," IES NCES, n.d., https://nces.ed.gov/programs/digest/d20/tables/dt20_326.10.asp?referer=raceindica.asp

2   IEC NCES, "Digest of Education Statistics, Table 326.10," IES NCES, n.d., https://nces.ed.gov/programs/digest/d20/tables/dt20_326.10.asp?referer=raceindica.asp

BFA – BACHELOR OF FINE ARTS

The Bachelor of Fine Arts is a 4-year college degree focusing on the arts. BFA students are often not required to take as many English, science, math, social science, and humanities courses. However, they must still complete roughly the same number of credits as a person who earns a BA or BS, and the courses are not necessarily easier. BFA students frequently take general art requirements to lay a foundation in drawing, graphic design, and courses in their specialty area during their first two years, along with basic writing and quantitative skill-building.

BFA students are traditionally art-in-practice students who learn the technical craft of their art form while putting in enormous numbers of hours practicing their skill doing assignments and participating in internships and experiential learning. Students who know that they want a future in the arts often find this avenue perfectly tailored for their pursuits. However, students who change their minds and transfer to a university in another degree program may require an additional year to make up for coursework they have not completed.

MFA – MASTER OF FINE ARTS

The Master of Fine Arts is a graduate degree for students who have completed their BA, BS, or BFA. This degree takes one to two years depending upon the program, coursework, and experiential component, which may be a capstone, practicum, internship, or thesis. While there are also MA and MS degrees, many art students who continue to earn their master's degree in the arts chose to focus on their field of interest. The MFA is an intensive immersion into a higher level of skill-building. However, students who graduate with an MFA have a broader range of talents and experiences than those who earn their bachelor's degrees. While admission into these programs is generally selective, with planning, preparation, and a good portfolio, there are options for you to pursue your interests.

THE SEVEN MAJOR DIFFERENCES BETWEEN THE ASSOCIATE, BACHELORS, AND MASTER'S DEGREES

1. Starting Point
2. Academic Discipline
3. Time to Completion
4. Location of the Education
5. Educational Costs
6. Earning Power
7. Professional Opportunities

STARTING POINT

Most students who begin with an Associate of Arts (AA) or Associate of Science (AS) have no college credits. Starting from scratch with their college education, they accumulate their 60+ units beginning from this community college starting point. While most students earn AA or AS degrees at a community college, some earn this degree at a 4-year college or university.

The AA or AS is either a terminal degree, meaning that the student will not continue on with their bachelor's degree or just a steppingstone to their BA, BS, or BFA. The difference between the associate's and bachelor's degrees is just the starting point.

The starting point for students who pursue a bachelor's degree may be farther along the traditional 4-year pathway. Meanwhile, the starting point for the master's degree (MA, MS, or MFA) begins after obtaining a bachelor's degree.

ACADEMIC DISCIPLINE

Every degree encompasses different requirements. Since the requirements for a chemistry degree are not the same as for biology and a degree in illustration differs from, for example, photography, the course requirements for different majors may include different numbers of credits as well as different classes and competencies. The MA, MS, and MFA build upon the bachelor's degree and dive even deeper. Illustration majors will not always take the same classes as those in fine arts or graphic design, though a few may overlap. Both are essential to the arts. However, these two career areas are distinct. Thus, the course requirements are also unique.

Furthermore, with the myriad of combinations, it is rare that any two undergraduate students have the same exact classes in the same exact order. Since the requirements for a chemistry degree are not the same as for biology and a degree in illustration differs from, for example, photography, the course requirements for different majors may include different numbers of credits as well as different classes and competencies.

TIME TO COMPLETION

Associate of Arts (AA) and Associate of Science (AS) degrees typically take two years, while most BA, BS, and BFA degrees are 4-year programs, depending upon full-time or part-time status. Students who transfer in credits or earn credits otherwise can reduce their time to completion.

Some students may choose to extend their education in illustration and comic art by earning a second bachelor's degree in another field. By cross-training in film, animation, or marketing, students open more doors. Additionally, a degree in business on the bachelor's level or Master's in Business Administration (MBA) may lead to alternative leadership positions.

Time in college can be reduced. Some students enter a BA, BS, or BFA program having already completed college credits because they were dual-enrolled or they took college classes directly through a college or university ahead of time. Some students have taken AP/IB tests from taking higher-level classes while in high school and earned qualifying scores to be granted credits by the college or university. Other ways students can enter at a different starting point are with credit-by-exam, CLEP tests, experiential credits, and those granted in the military.

Colleges and universities are keenly aware of the challenges students face today with work, illness, and family responsibilities. Thus, many schools of higher education offer flexible enrollment with opportunities for part-time, evening, weekend, and online classes.

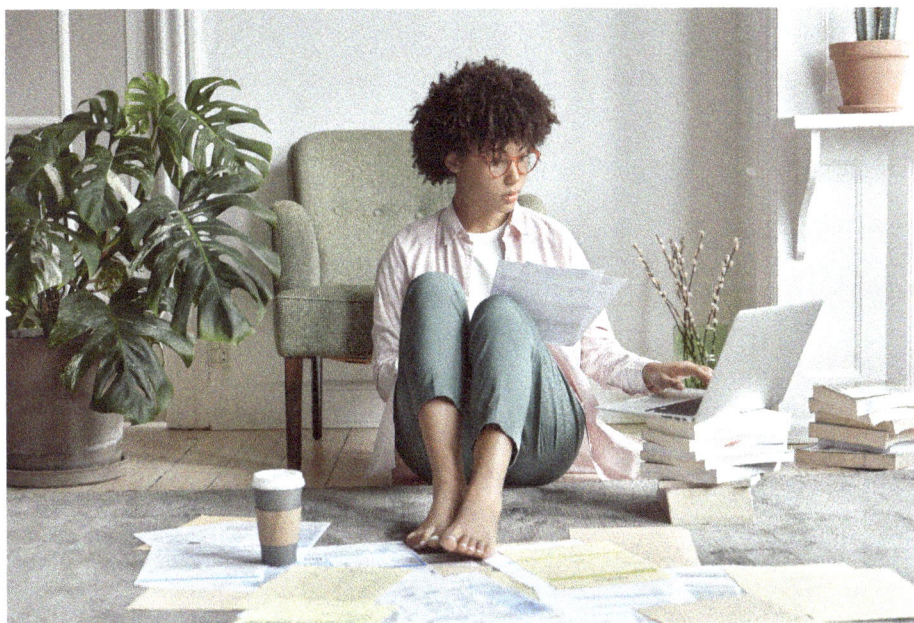

LOCATION OF THE EDUCATION

The AA and AS are earned at colleges that grant 2-year degrees. The location may be at a local community college or a university. BA, BS, and BFA programs are offered at a 4-year college or university. However, with online classes, students have the flexibility to take classes from colleges farther away as well. Thus, the location in which a typical student studies is not as set as it once was. Nevertheless, the in-person internships are often situated in corporate hubs and thus require grounding to a specific location.

EDUCATIONAL COSTS

Since the AA or AS requires a shorter amount of time and is typically completed at a lower-cost community college, the cost for an associate's degree is typically less than a bachelor's degree. Master's degree programs cost more per credit but take less time than a bachelor's degree.

On the other hand, many students can obtain financial aid in the form of grants, loans, and both merit and need-based scholarships. This aid can pay for school and reduce debt after college.

EARNING POWER

Students with more education can earn more. According to the 2019 National Center for Educational Statistics (NCES) data for the median person,[3]

Master's Degree or Higher - $70,000

Bachelor's Degree - $55,700

Associate's Degree - $43,300

High School - $35,000

Of course, there is a wide range in annual salaries from those who have consistent work and are paid six-digit or seven-digit salaries to those who work one or two paid shows per year and earn less than $20,000. Thus, the average seems low when the variation is huge.

PROFESSIONAL OPPORTUNITIES

Earning a BA, BS, or BFA opens more doors than an AA or AS. Similarly, an MA,

---

3   IES NCES, "Annual Earnings by Educational Attainment," IEC NCES, May 2021, https://nces.ed.gov/programs/coe/indicator/cba

MS, or MFA opens more doors than a BA, BS, or BFA. Baccalaureate and master's degrees require more training. You can obtain this training through workshops or studio classes, but with a scholarship to pay for college, you might find that the training and opportunities are worth your time. Besides, you will gain additional skills that could prove valuable in your future.

VERBEELDING
Van de Baay en Havens van
VIGOS,
met de verovering der
FRANSCHE OORLOGS~EN
SPAANSCHE ZILVERVLOOT

CHAPTER 7

COLLEGE ADMISSIONS: APPLICATIONS, ESSAYS, RECOMMENDATIONS, AND FINANCIAL AID

"The object of art is not to reproduce reality, but to create a reality of the same intensity."

– Alberto Giacometti

RISD, SVA, Cal Arts, NYU, and SAIC stand out for illustration, comic book, or cartooning programs with amazing faculty, excellent facilities, and easy access to internships. While most students consider New York City for the top college art programs and internships, they should not discount other major metropolitan areas like Chicago and Los Angeles as well as cities around the country that are meccas for artists and journalists. However, you cannot go wrong going to RISD for its deep dive into the world of art. These colleges offer a rigorous course of study and socially responsible projects on the cutting edge of art, design, and forward-thinking optimism.

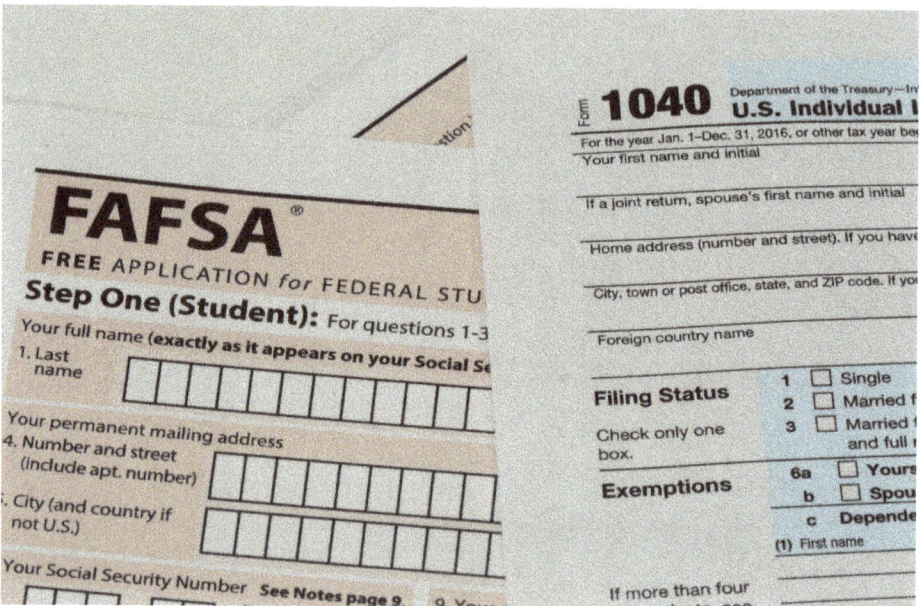

SCHOLARSHIPS

Nearly every university in the United States offers need-based scholarships. Apply by submitting the Free Application for Federal Student Aid (FAFSA) found at www.studentaid.gov. Some colleges also require the College Scholarship Service (CSS) Profile which is available on the College Board website at www.collegeboard.org. Additionally, most colleges also offer merit scholarships. Please check out the profile section. Below are six schools chosen at random to give you a sense of the options listed in the profile section.

Act as if what you do makes a difference. It does.

- William James

ArtCenter College of Design

ArtCenter offers more than $22 million in scholarships for students with need and talent each year. Amounts vary based on need, talent, available funds, and recommendations from the scholarship committee. ArtCenter offers continuing scholarships for students currently in school.

Columbia College Chicago

Columbia College offers merit and need-based scholarships to more than a hundred freshmen, transfer, and graduate students. Most of the scholarships are renewable each year with given GPA and coursework requirements. Columbia College meets four years of full-need of both domestic and international applicants. For merit scholarships, creative samples must be submitted with the application. Full tuition awards are also available.

Pratt Institute

Pratt offers generous merit-based scholarships. Sixty percent of incoming first-year students are offered merit-based awards for their talent. In addition, Pratt has restricted and endowed scholarships along with its need-based financial aid program. International students are also eligible for merit-based awards. No additional application is required for prospective students; all admitted students are considered automatically.

Rhode Island School of Design

RISD offers scholarships to students who demonstrate academic and talent-based success and financial need. Many students receive $20,000 awards. However, scholarships are need-based, and international students must pay the full tuition.

Savannah College of Art and Design (SCAD)

Some colleges are exceptionally generous with money for a large proportion of students. For example, at SCAD, 80% of new applicants receive merit & need-based scholarships. These opportunities are available for U.S. citizens, permanent residents, and international students.

Syracuse University

Syracuse University students received more than $400 million in financial aid. Syracuse offers internal merit-based scholarships and supports students in finding external funds as well. Merit-based funding is offered to more than 35% of the incoming class. Approximately 80% of SU's incoming students received some type of financial support. Syracuse University offers a financial aid package to incoming students that meet full-need.

COLLEGE ADMISSIONS:

Success in the Face of Uncertainty

There are no guarantees in college admissions. However, planning is essential for success. The most beneficial advice is to pursue your passions with gusto, train to be the best you can be, take advantage of internships and experiences, and meet lots of people along the way.

Remember, "life is a journey, not a destination." Often the journey is more exciting, leading to lessons, friendships, and unforgettable moments. However, the fact is, in the end, if college is your goal, then you need to know a few action items to remember for success.

Should you worry about grades? Of course. You should also take classes that will challenge you. Colleges pick the best candidates from those who apply. Students must be academically prepared, socially conscious, and talented in a few different areas in which they are passionate (design, graphic arts, musical instruments, theatre, debate, public speaking, leadership, athletics, community service, computer coding, robotics, construction, etc.).

The college selection process is not that much different than companies picking employees. While colleges are more or less competitive, companies may have only one job, and a hundred resumes. Discover the unique drive and internal motivations within you that make you the very best you can be. Be exceptional at what you choose to do academically, personally, and professionally.

Most of all, You Do You

TALENT FOCUSED

Not all schools require high grades and test scores. Many are simply interested in selecting students who are the most talented, most driven, and the most willing to be team players on the college campus. Thus, while you should take a solid set of courses and fulfill the standard requirements, only the top schools emphasize completing a challenging curriculum while earning high grades and standardized test scores.

FOR HIGHLY SELECTIVE COLLEGES, TALENT IS JUST THE BEGINNING

A few highly selective colleges seek extraordinary talent over academics, but most zero in on a student's challenging courses and high grades. To gain admission into the most highly selective academic colleges, you must take the most challenging course load you can manage and succeed. Highly selective colleges want disciplined scholars AND remarkably talented students.

Determine what you can handle, knowing that some colleges with extremely competitive admissions standards will only take students who have completed more than ten AP, IB, or honors classes over the four years.

Why would these most competitive colleges require these classes? However daunting these classes may seem, remember, the top colleges have lots of applicants, and they need to draw the line somewhere. UCLA had 149,779 applicants for fall 2022; UC Berkeley had 128,192 applicants. The numbers are truly staggering since neither first-year class will not have more than 7,000 students starting in the fall.

College admissions can feel like a rollercoaster of energy and emotion. Creating a portfolio of talent, training, and experience is just the beginning. Meanwhile, some colleges want to see standardized test scores aided by practice. Applications and essays may seem easy at first, but managing the various requirements and deadlines can be difficult. Therefore, this moment is a good time to get a calendar and organize your tasks.

REQUEST INFORMATION

Almost every college has a location, a link, or a 'contact us' page where you can request information from the school. If you are considering a school, request information from them. In this way, they may send you updates, scholarship opportunities, a valuable application fee waiver, special invites, and other information that could be valuable in the process. Of course, you may not need one more e-mail, and you may be receiving e-mails from the school anyway. Still, I recommend that you fill out their form. Then, since you are likely to be inundated with e-mails, make a file folder in your e-mail for all colleges you are considering. Then, when you get an e-mail from one of those schools, file it away.

STANDARDIZED TESTING

A few schools still require standardized testing. Check first. Many colleges are test-optional. This means that you are not required to take the SAT or ACT. However, if you have a good score, it may make all the difference in gaining admission. College admissions offices are studying this topic and considering their future policies. Much of their concern began with test cancelations worldwide due to the pandemic.

Schools did not want to let students into their site to take the test who may be infected, nor were they able to ensure safety. In addition, social distancing requirements limited the number of students who could take a test at any given site. Yet, for decades, college admissions decisions centered around grades and test scores. This change in the landscape of decision-making has rattled admissions departments.

Meanwhile, some colleges proclaim that 'test-optional' truly means that the test is not required. Yet, evidence proves otherwise. Yet, evidence proves otherwise. Thus, many students are still taking the test and working around the hurdles amid the confusion. Competition continues to drive students to present evidence to show that they are worthy candidates. In the end, colleges need to make a final decision between very good candidates. If one student has a high score, that student may have a higher likelihood of admission depending upon the admissions committee's decision-making process.

Data show that students who submitted scores within the college's range or higher were accepted at a higher rate than those without a score. Some schools are test blind in that they say that they do not consider your scores. A few of these colleges still provide a place to input your scores. Thus, they are not truly blind. Nevertheless, the decision regarding whether you take the test or submit the score is yours. If the school does not require an admissions test, you can choose to take the test and submit it as you like. If your academics are solid and you are willing to prepare for the test, you should take the test.

APPLYING EARLY

Early Action (EA), Restricted Early Action (REA), and Early Decision (ED)

With low acceptance rates, the chance to get more scholarship money, and chaos surrounding the cancellations and changes in AP, IB, SAT, and ACT testing, students clamor to apply early to schools. In addition, applications to the top schools increased during the pandemic, resulting in colleges needing to make difficult admissions decisions in their quest to build a diverse, talented, and engaged class of students. Furthermore, students applying early have access to many more scholarship options. This confluence sent students in droves to apply early. This trend is likely to continue.

In Early Action (EA), Restricted Early Action (REA), and Early Decision (ED), students apply in late summer or early fall to college and generally find out around winter break, though some decisions come out earlier and a few arrive later. This advantage not only gives students a chance for more scholarship money in some cases but the benefit of finding out early reduces the tension of the long waiting period to find out about Regular Decision schools.

Early Action (EA) and Restricted Early Action (REA) are different. In restricted early action, a limitation is placed on either how many or what colleges you can apply to simultaneously. Many REA schools do not allow students to apply to other early action schools, though some will allow students to apply early to public colleges. Check the colleges to be sure. In addition, some schools like Georgetown will allow students to apply EA elsewhere but not apply to a binding Early Decision (ED) program where the student commits to attending if they are accepted. However, most EA schools do not have these restrictions, and some students apply to a handful of EA schools during the admissions process.

Early Decision (ED) is a binding agreement between the student and college with signatures from the student's parents and the high school assuring that the student is committed and will attend. Each of these parties acknowledges and agrees that, if granted admission, they will fulfill their agreement. There are caveats to this, though you should go into the agreement fully committing to your ED school.

There are incentives to applying ED. Frequently, acceptance rates are higher. Also, at some schools, a large percentage of their class is filled with students who profess their unequivocal love for their dream school. Students who know they have a top choice school, have the necessary admissions prerequisites fulfilled, and are committed to accepting the binding agreement to attend, should apply ED.

COMMON APPLICATION, COALITION APPLICATION, OR COLLEGE-SPECIFIC APPLICATION

Every college's process is unique. However, there are a few commonalities. In 2022, approximately 900 colleges used the Common App; about 150 colleges used the Coalition Application. A few used both. The University of California system has its own application as do the California State Universities and the Texas schools.

The Common App and Coalition App may be started early. In your junior year, consider getting a head start on reviewing what is required. The college-specific questions may change each year. However, the basic application is generally the same and can be created ahead of time. At the end of July, make a copy of everything you have completed just in case.

Some schools admit on a rolling basis. 'Rolling' means that periodically, after all of the materials are received, the admissions committee determines who they

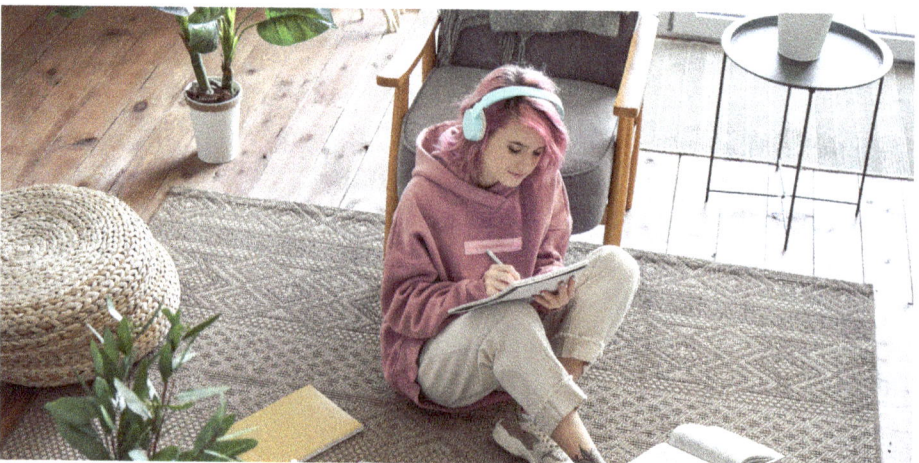

will accept, and they send the notification right away. Many students are accepted as early as August. The thrill of acceptance cannot be overstated.

ESSAYS

The Common Application and Coalition essays are often posted months ahead of time. Since this main essay is required or recommended for nearly all Common Application and Coalition Application schools, this is an excellent place to start thinking about what you might want to say to colleges.

In addition to the main essay on the Common Application and Coalition Application, about three-fours of the colleges have their own specific questions or essays. In August, most admissions applications are open and ready for you to dive into the college-specific questions, though many of the essay topics are available earlier, and some schools hold out until later for their big essay reveal.

These can be prepared ahead of time too. One popular question is, "What activity is most important to you and why?" Another is "Why did you choose your major?" A third common question is, "Why do you want to attend our school?" Others you should prepare or at least consider the topics of diversity, adversity, and challenges since these topics have become increasingly important in the admissions process. Everyone has a challenge they needed to overcome. What did you learn from that experience?

Complete the application fully. Think carefully about optional sections. Typically, universities offer you the chance to provide the school with just the right cherry on top of the ice cream sundae, allowing you to share something unique about you. If you have absolutely nothing to say, then leave it blank. There is an additional information section on the main Common App, Coalition Application, and University of California application. This location is not a place to write another essay, but you can include information that could not be adequately explained in the rest of the application.

There are also some schools that include scholarship essays within the supplement part of the application. Start early.

LETTERS OF RECOMMENDATION

Most colleges, though not all, request letters of recommendation from a counselor and one or more teachers. For illustration, comic book, or cartooning programs, the university may want academic teachers and art teachers. Plan for this. Occasionally, there is a section for optional recommendations too. In this location, you might get a recommendation from a summer program leader or someone with whom you did an internship. If you were in a sport, there is a location for a coach on about a quarter of the applications. Finally, if there is a supplemental application, for example, on SlideRoom, these often require separate recommendations reviewed by the art program.

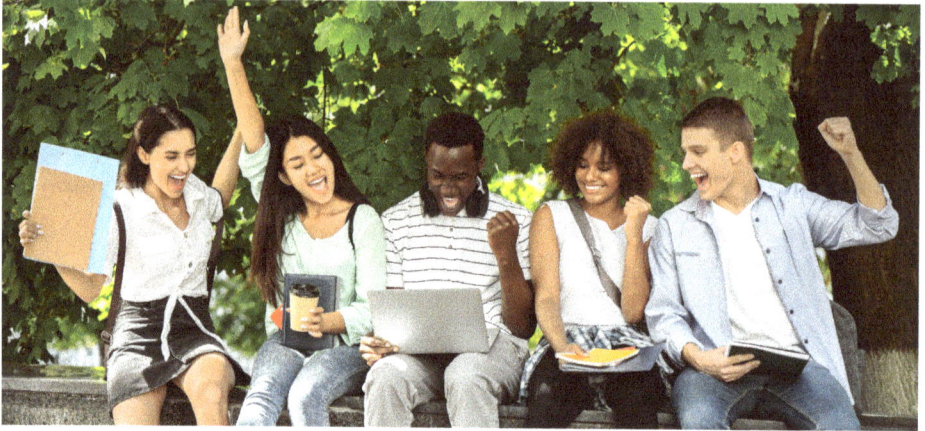

DECISIONS, DECISIONS: WAITING FOR A RESPONSE

The period between submitting your application and getting your admissions results may not require a tremendous amount of work, but it does require patience and diligence. First, most schools will send you a link to a portal where you will check your results, though the most important reason for checking every couple of weeks is to ensure that the college is not missing something or has not offered you the chance to apply for an extra scholarship.

Check your portal regularly. Otherwise, read the college's correspondence sent through your e-mail. Waiting is difficult. These few months are a tough period because students want to know. However, the college typically lists the date they will send out the results on the portal. Other popular sites post their decision notification dates too. You will find out soon.

CELEBRATING ACCEPTANCES AND DEALING WITH REJECTION

Acceptance is not guaranteed. The probabilities are low at the most highly selective schools. However, you just need to work hard in school to have what it takes and give this commitment to academics all you have. When you find out the results, you will celebrate your acceptances.

Congratulations! The colleges in which you gain admission go on your list of wins. Check your financial aid and scholarship packages too. Money is often an important factor in making your decision. Consider visiting the school. Many students apply to college merely by someone's recommendation, *U.S. News and World Report* ranking, looking at campus photos on Google, or researching profiles posted on a website or in a book.

There is nothing that replaces the actual campus visit. After all, you will be spending a few years there. While you may not be accepted everywhere you apply, you may decide when you visit that the college is high on your list or that you do not want to apply after all. Understandably, the pandemic's uncertainty added more question marks to an already complicated set of admissions processes.

The buzzword for 2020-2030 is resilience. It is never easy to be rejected. However, rejection happens, and you will survive this. Note that many colleges still accept applications in April, May, and June long after most schools' applications are closed. Look up those colleges if you did not get accepted or if you want to see what other schools might be good options for you. In April and May, Google "College Openings Update". You will be surprised to see the colleges that show up on the list that still have open spots.

WAITLISTS: THE ART OF WAITING

Immediately confirm if you are given a waitlist spot and still want to attend. There is often a deadline. You do not want to miss this. If you are no longer interested or have selected another school, go into the portal and turn down the offer. Someone else is bound to be thrilled by your anonymous gift.

If you are still interested, find the location on the portal or site designated by the college to update them on what you have done – accomplishments, awards, extra class, honors, art, shows, or films. You only want to add what they have not yet seen, but if you have taken the initiative to do something more than what you originally stated on the application, by all means, tell them.

You could just wait for their decision, but you are better off being proactive and showing that you really want to be at their school. Students do get off the waitlists at most schools. How much do you want to attend? Meanwhile, you will have to deposit somewhere else before the May 1st deadline. Stay hopeful. This next year will be a significant step along your journey. Relax!

CHAPTER 8

SUPPLEMENTAL MATERIALS AND PORTFOLIOS FOR ILLUSTRATION AND COMIC BOOK DESIGN PROGRAMS

"I'm a huge comic book collector. When I was a kid ... I was my own librarian. I made card files. I had origin stories of all the characters, and cross-referenced when they appeared in other comic books."

– James Mangold

Acceptance is very difficult at the top art and design schools like Rhode Island School of Design, School of Visual Arts, New York University, CalArts, Parsons School of Design, and School of the Art Institute of Chicago. Furthermore, the BFA degree is completely immersive. Inspired by the environment, you will be surrounded by students who are creative, multitalented, and focused.

Students must be wholly dedicated to art. Thus, admissions officers and art school directors are keenly interested in the applicant's talent and commitment. As a result, a portfolio review is required for the top schools; sometimes, an interview is part of the admissions process as well. Applicants must demonstrate ability and potential.

CHANGES IN THE APPLICANT DEMOGRAPHICS CHALLENGES ON THE ROAD AHEAD

COVID-19 shook students as well as admissions offices. Many studio-centered programs closed down or went online. International students left for their country of origin and classes at a distance could not provide the needed materials, space, and opportunities. Many quit and did not return.

Furthermore, some art programs completely shut down. Colleges faced a crisis. While some programs reopened after COVID-19 and some students returned, demographic shifts resulted, including gender diversity and ethnic makeup. Additionally, the decreased population of international students shook art programs. Nevertheless, many students still applied.

Other challenges existed as well. COVID-19 changed the makeup of applicants to college. Other data show that while enrollments rebounded, some programs suffered from budget cuts.

NATIONAL PORTFOLIO DAYS

These online and in-person national events are free for students to participate anywhere they are located in the world. In-person events are often held both inside and outside of the United States. Prospective art program applicants have the chance to meet admissions staff and present art pieces. Students must register online. There are filters with the online registration so you can sign up for events that fit your needs: online in-person, undergraduates, transfer, or graduate school.

In-person events can be jam-packed with people, though COVID-19 changed procedures with limited numbers of individuals inside venues. In the past, massive

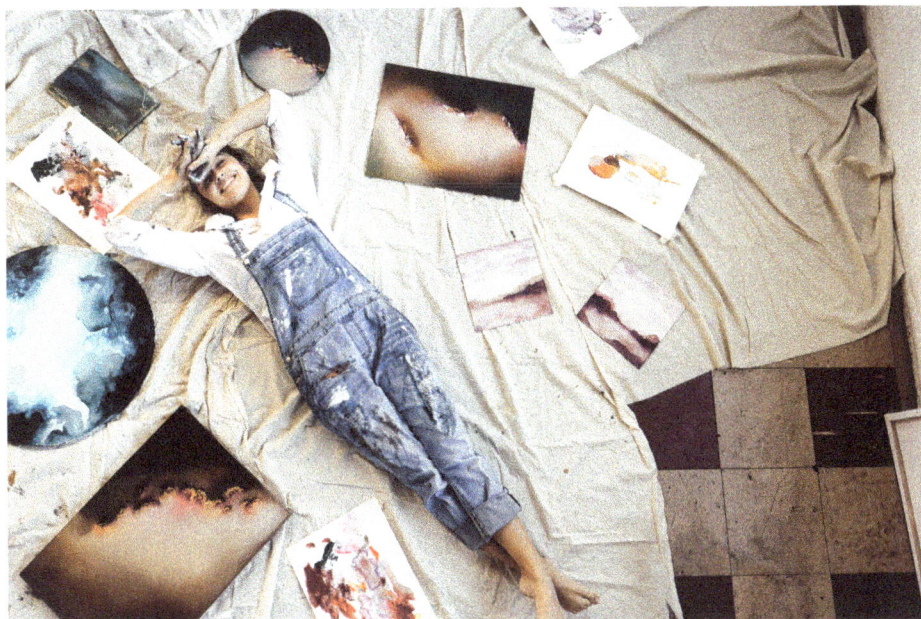

lines where students waited for their turn sometimes resulted in disappointed latecomers. In some locations, now, there is a reservation system. Make sure you read about any required protocols for in-person events.

More than fifty colleges come to many of the in-person events. Typically, you will have 10 to 15 minutes to speak to a representative and show them your work. You should bring a range of pieces. The website recommends bringing 10 – 12 pieces. Even if you only bring five, you are fine. The point is for your work to be reviewed so you can gain valuable feedback and improve.

For the online events, there are live sessions where you wait in a 'waiting room' queue until you can be seen. You can also schedule a meeting, though only on the day of the event. You may register for multiple school reviews. Note that you will not upload your portfolio. Rather, you will meet with your reviewer via Zoom and share your screen.

These events do not guarantee admission, and no admissions decisions are made at these events. In addition, although the colleges may suggest that you apply for their scholarships or you may be considered for their merit awards, you will not be awarded any money at these events.

In most cases, you will still need to present your portfolio online through the school-determined application portal. Even so, these events are excellent in that they allow you to meet people from various colleges and they get a chance to meet you. Furthermore, you get helpful advice and suggestions on how you can improve the pieces you plan to submit.

ART SCHOOL ADMISSIONS

RISD offers its own portfolio days online, where they will review your work and give you a valuable critique. Hint: RISD looks for engaged learners who will connect with the world. They want art that says something meaningful, evokes emotion, and shares a point of view. Being technically strong is essential, but being emotionally strong and inextricably linked to the audience is imperative. Thus, more is not better. Only share your best work.

Portfolios are required at many art colleges. Since students often apply to 10-20 schools, the effort can be daunting. Furthermore, completing applications and creating portfolios take time and money for training, preparation, application fees, and other expenses.

PORTFOLIO REQUIREMENTS

The first entry point to art programs is to investigate programs. Apply to your dream school, but also select colleges that have programs that fit your criteria – classes, program requirements, geography, studio space, faculty, career prospects, cost, etc. For now, let's look at the portfolio requirements at a few schools. Start by getting a general idea of what each school requires so that you are prepared. More information is provided in the profiles later on in this book.

CALIFORNIA INSTITUTE OF THE ARTS

BFA Character Animation
(CalArts does not offer Illustration)

The focus of this program is storytelling. Students must have originality, life drawing skills, and the ability to use sequential imagery. Portfolio submissions may include drawings, traditional art, digital art, and computer graphics. After completing the CalArts application and artist statement, applicants must submit artwork (minimum of 15 with life drawings), a sketchbook (inspirations and drawings), and a video introduction (30-90 seconds).

PARSONS SCHOOL OF ART AND DESIGN

BFA Illustration; BFA Communication Design

Parsons requests an uploaded portfolio of eight to twelve images from a student's breadth of media skills, including drawing, painting, sculpture, design, collage, animation, etc. Experimentation, imagination, and self-expression are key. Include documentation and descriptions of your work and process. Parsons also requires a submission called "The Parsons Challenge". Start this part early. Many students put this off, and either does a lackluster job or cannot pull this together before the deadline. The Parsons Challenge is a new visual work inspired by a theme expressed in work within the portfolio. Students submit a required 500-word essay describing the development of the idea. Two additional pieces may be added to document your process. Observational work is not required since technique and vision are emphasized in the review.

NEW YORK UNIVERSITY

BFA Studio Art

After completing the Common Application, students will submit an "Artistic Review" from your application status page. Media uploads can include images of artwork (drawing, painting, sculpture, video, photography, digital art, etc.) that represent your artistic interests while also demonstrating your technical abilities and imagination. You must include 12-15 images of recent artwork in any medium. You will also present a one-page "Statement of Purpose".

RHODE ISLAND SCHOOL OF DESIGN

BFA Illustration; BFA Graphic Design

After completing the Common Application, students will submit a SlideRoom supplement. Students present 12-20 examples of their recent artwork on the SlideRoom site. RISD requests finished pieces, drawings from direct observation, and no more than three pieces that show research and prep work. RISD's admissions are competitive, so you should curate and edit the pieces you choose to submit in your portfolio.

SCHOOL OF THE ART INSTITUTE OF CHICAGO

BFA Art & Technology Studies
BFA Printmedia
BFA Visual Communication Design

Submit the Common Application, noting the merit scholarship deadlines and specific requirements. All programs require a SlideRoom portfolio. Develop the 250-500-word artist's statement describing how and why you created the pieces you submitted and how your experiences contributed to your thinking. Include 10-15 creative works that demonstrate your potential from observational to abstract.

All media are considered, though SAIC suggests submitting those that are bold, inventive, thought-provoking, expressive, and risk-taking. You may concentrate on a single media or any combination of drawings, prints, photographs, paintings, film, video, audio recordings, sculpture, ceramics, fashion designs, graphic design, furniture, objects, architectural designs, websites, video games, sketchbooks, scripts, storyboards, screenplays, and zines.

SCHOOL OF VISUAL ARTS

BFA Cartooning; BFA Illustration;
BFA Computer Art, Computer Animation, & Visual Effects

Apply through the SVA site and submit a portfolio of 15-20 images of your strongest artwork through Slideroom. Include samples of your drawing with a minimum of 3-5 examples from direct observation (self-portraits, figure drawings, object studies, still life, and landscape). Other media, like painting, photography, printmaking, collage, etc., are welcome. Sketchbooks, shown at in-person reviews, offer valuable insights. For cartooning and illustration, share your personal interests, graphic novels, or strips, though do not overload the portfolio with comics or cartoon characters. You need to be able to take people, places, and things from the real world into a two-dimensional picture. Thus, direct observational work is essential to include.

Upper left figure (posterior thigh, left):

lutæa superior (ramus superior)

Sciatic artery
A. glutæa inferior

Internal pudic
artery² — A. pudenda interna
reat sacrosciatic ligament
cerosum
rior hæmorrhoidal artery⁹
æmorrhoidalis inferior

omes nervi ischiadici
—A. comitans n. ischiadici

Adductor magnus muscle

Semitendinosus muscle

flexor cruris muscle (long head)
ps femoris (caput longum)

Semitendinosus muscle

Adductor magnus muscle

Popliteal vein — V. poplitea
dductor magnus muscle through which
els pass into the popliteal space, form-
erior orifice of Hunter's canal (†)
Semimembranosus muscle
rnus muscle — M. vastus medialis
Superior internal articular artery
A. genu superior medialis
al sural artery⁵ — A. suralis medialis
astrocnemius muscle (inner head)
. gastrocnemius (caput mediale)
Inferior internal articular
artery — A. genu inferior medialis
Popliteal vein — V. poplitea
Internal popliteal nerve
N. tibialis

) Hiatus tendineus (adductorius)

Pyriformis muscle — M. pyri
Inferior gluteal nerve
N. gluteus inferior

Obturator internus muscle
gemellus superior muscle
the gemellus inferior m

Trochanteric rete¹
Rete trochantericum
Internal circumflex ar
"deep branch²—A. ci
medialis ("ramu
Quadratus femoris mu

Offset of the first or
perforating artery —
arteria perforantis
Gluteus maximus m
M. gluteus maximus
Adductor minimus m

First or superior perfor
A. perforans prima

Superior medullary or nutri
the femur⁴ — A. nutricia fe
External intermuscular sept
Septum intermusculare (fem
Third or inferior perforating
A. perforans tertia
Biceps flexor cruris muscle (
M. biceps femoris (caput bre
Muscular branch of the fe
Ramus muscularis arteriae
Inferior medullary or nut
the femur⁴ — A. nutricia
Biceps flexor cruris musc
M. biceps femoris (caput

Muscular branch
Ramus muscularis
Superior external articular arter
A. genu superior lateralis
External sural artery⁵
A. suralis lateralis
Middle or azygos articular arte
A. genu media
Gastrocnemius muscle (outer he
M. gastrocnemius (caput latera
Plantaris muscle
Inferior external articular artery
A. genu inferior lateralis
External popliteal, or peroneal, ne
N. peroneus communis
Tendinous arch of the soleus muscl
Arcus tendineus m. solei

Upper right figure (posterior thigh/leg, right):

Gluteus maximus muscle
M. gluteus maximus

Gluteal artery (superior branch)¹
A. glutæa superior (ramus superior)

Internal pudic artery
A. pudenda interna
s of the sciatic artery which per-
the great sacrosciatic ligament
Arteriæ glutæa inferioris qui liga-
tum sacrotuberosum perforant
Pudic nerve — N. pudendus
Sciatic artery — A. glutæa inferior
imierary sciatic artery, which per-
es the great sciatic nerve (var.)
latus inferior additus qui nervum
ischiadicum perforat

Comes nervi ischiadici artery
A. comitans n. ischiadici

Gracilis muscle

Adductor magnus muscle

Semimembranosus muscle

Deep fascia of the thigh, or fascia lata
(cut off short, and turned outwards)

Semitendinosus muscle

Popliteal vein
V. poplitea

Popliteal artery
A. poplitea

Semimembranosus muscle

Internal popliteal nerve
N. tibialis

Gastrocnemius muscle (inner head)
M. gastrocnemius (caput mediale)
Internal sural artery
A. suralis medialis

Superficial sural artery
Ramus cutaneus arteriae
suralis medialis

Gluteus medius muscle
M. gluteus medius

Pyriformis muscle
M. pyriformis

Inferior gluteal nerve
N. gluteus inferior
Obturator internus and
gemelli muscles muscle
Great trochanter
Trochanter major
Internal circumflex
branch
A. circumflexa fem
"ramus pro
Quadratus femoris

Cutaneous offsets
superior perfora
Ramus cutaneus arter
prima

Cutaneous offsets of th
forating arteries ex
Rami cutanei arteriae
tium aliarum (serie

Great sciatic nerve
N. ischiadicus

Biceps flexor cruris muscle
M. biceps femoris

External popliteal or peronea
N. peroneus communis

External sural artery
A. suralis lateralis

Gastrocnemius muscle (outer he
M. gastrocnemius (caput latera

Lower left figure (anterior foot/ankle, dorsum):

Anterior tibial artery
A. tibialis anterior
seous membrane, or
ament, of the leg
ana interossea cruris
eal artery
ns arteriæ peroneæ
ommunicating branch
Ramus communicans
nal malleolar artery⁴
anterior lateralis
al malleolar rete⁵
malleolare laterale
nal tarsal artery
rsea lateralis
s digitorum pedis
uscle
digitorum brevis

l rete of the foot
orsale pedis

rating arteries⁷
es

rating arteries⁷
s

Tendon of the t
Tendo musculi

Anterior intern
A. malleolaris a

Internal mall
Rete malleol

Dorsal artery
A. dorsalis pe

Internal ta
Aa. tarsea

Metatar
A. arcu

Comm
(
Ram
Dorsal
Aa. m

Dor
Aa.

Lower right figure (plantar foot):

Calcaneal rete¹
Rete calcaneum

Internal plantar artery
A. plantaris medialis
Abductor hallucis muscle

"Deep branch"
"Ramus profundus"
"Superficial branch"
"Ramus superficialis"

or brevis digitorum pedis
muscle¹
flexor digitorum brevis

ndon of the flexor longus
hallucis muscle
or brevis hallucis muscle
exor hallucis brevis

Lumbricales muscles
Mm. lumbricales

imon¹ plantar digital
arteries¹
metatarseæ plantares

ial transverse ligament
of the toes
i transversi aponeurosis
plantaris

lateral¹ plantar digital
arteries¹
a. digitales plantares

External plantar artery
A. plantaris lateralis
Abductor minimi digiti pe
muscle
M. abductor digiti quin

Flexor brevis minimi di
muscle
M. flexor digiti minim
Interosseous muscles
Mm. interossei

Adductor transversus h
muscle
M. adductor hallucis
(transversum)

Anterior perforatin
Rami anastomotici a
digitalium plantariu
teris metatarseis di

CHAPTER 9

POST PANDEMIC EMPLOYMENT OUTLOOK: STATISTICS AND ECONOMIC PROJECTIONS

"When the temperature falls to zero, I curl up by the fire with a good book and for a while, I am a superhero."

– Rick Springfield

A rtists often enter many different fields and play essential roles in society. According to the *Occupational Outlook Handbook*, employment opportunities in these fields are slated to grow from 2020 to 2030 at different rates with new jobs expected. The median annual wage for entry-level positions is given below. The job outlook for artists is good with a 14% growth rate. Wages are also likely to increase.

According to the 2022 Bureau of Labor Statistics,[1]

OCCUPATION	JOB SUMMARY	ENTRY-LEVEL EDUCATION	MEDIAN PAY
Advertising Sales and Agents	Advertising sales agents sell advertising space to businesses and individuals.	High School Diploma or Equivalent	$52,340
Archivists, Curators, and Museum Workers	Archivists and curators oversee institutions' collections, such as historical items or of artwork. Museum technicians and conservators prepare and restore items in those collections.	Varies	$50,120
Art Directors	Art directors are responsible for the visual style and images in magazines, newspapers, product packaging, and movie and television productions.	Bachelor's Degree	$100,890
Broadcast, Sound, and Video Technicians	Broadcast, sound, and video technicians set up, operate, and maintain the electrical equipment for media programs.	Varies	$49,050
Craft and Fine Artists	Craft and fine artists use a variety of materials and techniques to create art for sale and exhibition.	Varies	$49,960
Dancers and Choreographers	Dancers and choreographers use dance performances to express ideas and stories.	Varies	N/A
Desktop Publishers	Desktop publishers use computer software to design page layouts for items that are printed or published online.	Associate's Degree	$46,910

---

1   Bureau of Labor Statistics, U.S. Department of Labor, *Occupational Outlook Handbook*, Craft and Fine Artists, at https://www.bls.gov/ooh/arts-and-design/craft-and-fine-artists.htm.

OCCUPATION	JOB SUMMARY	ENTRY-LEVEL EDUCATION	MEDIAN PAY
Editors	Editors plan, review, and revise content for publication.	Bachelor's Degree	$63,350
Fashion Designers	Fashion designers create clothing, accessories, and footwear.	Bachelor's Degree	$77,450
Film and Video Editors & Camera Operators	Film and video editors and camera operators manipulate moving images that entertain or inform an audience.	Bachelor's Degree	$60,360
Graphic Designers	Graphic designers create visual concepts, using computer software or by hand, to communicate ideas that inspire, inform, and captivate consumers.	Bachelor's Degree	$50,710
Industrial Designers	Industrial designers combine art, business, and engineering to develop the concepts for manufactured products.	Bachelor's Degree	$77,030
Jewelers & Precious Stone & Metal Workers	Jewelers and precious stone and metal workers design, construct, adjust, repair, appraise and sell jewelry.	Bachelor's Degree	$46,640
Market Research Analysts	Market research analysts study market conditions to examine potential sales of a product or service.	Bachelor's Degree	$63,920
News Analysts, Reporters, and Journalists	News analysts, reporters, and journalists keep the public updated about current events and noteworthy information.	Bachelor's Degree	$48,370
Postsecondary Teachers	Postsecondary teachers instruct students in a variety of academic subjects beyond the high school level.	Master's Degree	$79,640
Producers and Directors	Producers and directors make business and creative decisions about film, television, stage, and other productions.	Bachelor's Degree	$79,000

OCCUPATION	JOB SUMMARY	ENTRY-LEVEL EDUCATION	MEDIAN PAY
Public Relations & Fundraising Managers	Public relations managers direct the creation of materials that will enhance the public image of their employer or client. Fundraising managers coordinate campaigns that bring in donations for their organization.	Bachelor's Degree	$119,860
Public Relations Specialists	Public relations specialists create and maintain a positive public image for the clients they represent.	Bachelor's Degree	$62,800
Sales Managers	Sales managers direct organizations' sales teams.	Bachelor's Degree	$127,490
Photographers	Photographers use their technical expertise, creativity, and composition skills to produce and preserve images.	Bachelor's Degree	$38,950
Special Effects Artists & Animators	Special effects artists and animators create images that appear to move and visual effects for various forms of media and entertainment.	Bachelor's Degree	$78,790
Technical Writers	Technical writers prepare instruction manuals, how-to guides, journal articles, and other supporting documents to communicate complex and technical information more easily.	Bachelor's Degree	$78,060
Woodworkers	Woodworkers manufacture a variety of products, such as cabinets and furniture, using wood, veneers, and laminates.	High School Diploma or Equivalent	$36,710
Writers and Authors	Writers and authors develop written content for various types of media.	Bachelor's Degree	$67,120

We know what we are but know not what we may be.

– William Shakespeare

Artists work in studios where they immortalize ideas in a job that is a cross between artist, Imagineer, and digital content expert. The median pay for an artist is $49,120 with a bachelor's degree. Those with a master's degree are typically paid higher due to their more specialized, focused knowledge. The employment prospects for artists are positive with 7,000 new jobs expected in 2022.

Similar jobs, listed in the previous chart, vary across subjects since artists have different focuses. The fluidity and opportunity in art across travel, nature, marketing, journalism, and fashion run the gamut of options, not to mention portrait work. Society has a wide and varied use for the skills of an artist. However, you will need to discover your personal areas of interest.

The skills an art student learns in school, including drawing, painting, graphic design, printmaking, package design, illustration, comic book art, collage, sculpture, ceramics, crafts, and computer-aided design are valuable and transferrable to other fields as well. According to the Bureau of Labor Statistics, approximately 54% of artists are self-employed while 7% work in the federal government, 7% in independent jobs, 5% in the motion picture and sound recording industries, and 3% work in personal care services.[2]

IMPACT OF COVID-19

COVID-19 impacted the number of jobs people could get in art. A significant drop in opportunities led most artists to the internet to post their art and set up their independent work for freelancing. The dynamic changed as Pinterest, Instagram, and Facebook became inundated with images. One of my friends in the publishing business said that freelancers needed a "megaphone" or "gimmick"

2   Bureau of Labor Statistics, U.S. Department of Labor, *Occupational Outlook Handbook*, Craft and Fine Artists, at https://www.bls.gov/ooh/arts-and-design/craft-and-fine-artists.htm.

to get noticed. He is not a gimmicky kind of guy, so he searches for platforms to broadcast his work. Thus, the impact of COVID-19 cannot be understated. While the field is booming with more entrants presenting what they created, practicing continues to be essential, and technique can always be improved.

ROAD TO BECOMING AN ARTIST

The road to success in this industry should not be discouraging since a few steps are required along the way. Even so, achieving the goal is rewarding. Encourage those around you. If this is the field you want to pursue, pave the road in front of you and drive.

An internship or apprenticeship or two in peripheral areas would not hurt you in your pursuit of gigs and contract work. Although some internships are unpaid, you will find that most applicants will have one or more. Some internships pay fairly well. Even if you will ultimately be a freelancer, you might find parallel bread and butter professions while you fine-tune your craft.

If you are serious, you will make a fantastic career out of your pursuit. Initiative-taking persistence, talent, creativity, and moxie can get you into your desired college program and career. You may have to start at the very bottom of the ladder, but you can climb the rungs methodically one by one.

Companies want to know employees' work ethic, personality, and professionalism. An internship allows you to get to know the corporate climate better and allows others to get to know you better too. Thus, many companies hire the interns they feel are the best fit rather than choosing candidates from the piles of resumes that have been submitted.

Education unlocks doors no matter which direction your career takes you. Whatever direction you pursue, if you lay a foundation, undaunted by the competition, and are unafraid of starting at the bottom, you will do fine. Hard work and creativity go a long way in this industry. Start by getting a solid education.

MANAGEMENT AND EMPLOYEE RETENTION

Skills to Know: Management, Human Resources, Social Consciousness, Ethics

One of the most significant challenges facing employers in the years from 2022 - 2030 will be locating and retaining talent. The pandemic slowed education and learning with online classes, reduced access to faculty/advising, limited access to labs, inability to attend workshops, retail closures, and fewer conferences, meetings, and shows. Health concerns rose to the top of importance as did financial stress, job uncertainty, and social consciousness.

Many students chose to work rather than study and start online stores when they could not access locations for community service or continue with their sport, instrument, or hobbies. With the changes in lifestyle and fears about health, safety, and wellness, many bright and talented students developed a fearless sense of autonomy and independence, while for others, the necessary skills ordinarily developed in school were fraught by limitations.

Finding talent within the changing hiring atmosphere will require new skills to retain staff. Employees are increasingly looking elsewhere for a better opportunity. This development will require managers to earn and harness employee trust and loyalty.

The digital workforce has also placed demands on human resources. While many companies want their employees to work in-person, the convenience of working at home and the drudgery of commuting to work have created an environment where employees seek greater flexibility. Changes are coming. The employee talent challenge is likely to create a more global workforce where companies look for less expensive online talent from a pool of eager workers in other countries.

CHAPTER 10

NEXT STEPS: PREPARATION AND REAL-WORLD SKILLS

"Comics were always a way of creating and controlling and writing stories in which I was control of a world ... real family situations or real world situations. I think most kids tend to feel that they don't have any power so ... playing out the comic fantasy was the way to get that."

– Bill Sienkiewicz

Each illustration makes a lasting impression. As an illustrator, you will experience a dynamic, multidimensional world. In some careers, repetitive tasks and uninspiring projects lead employees to loathe their jobs and tick off minutes until their day is done. Yet, your life will undoubtedly be different and ever-changing since the world around you will change from moment to moment. Illustration and comic book design focus on creating, inventing, and energizing. Over time, whichever area of illustration becomes your focus, you will earn your way to a career of endless possibilities.

American neo-expressionist graffiti artist, Keith Haring, shared, "Art should be something that liberates your soul, provokes the imagination, and encourages people to go further." Today is a precious moment. As you contemplate college choices and tomorrow's future, you will explore your passion, open doors you never expected, and discover opportunities that will tantalize and challenge you along the way. You will also find ways to serve humanity. As such, you will capture a new, exciting, and eclectic way of life.

Contemplate your work, always critiquing yourself. You will enhance and uplift your world by adding intrigue. Spend time thinking, even though time sometimes seems short. You may feel as if time slips through your fingers like sand in an hourglass. Resist the temptation to post, remembering that imaginative, captivating characters and images move people deeply. While you can quickly post your artwork for the world to see, the truly magical pictures are created when time stands still, and you immerse yourself in a creative state.

Bring people into your world, allowing them to feel and interpret art in their unique way. Through comic books, you get to tell motivational stories each day which may make all the difference in a person's life. Societal purpose and technological innovation may change, though vision and service will never go out of style.

Attending a respected school can help you get noticed. Your next steps are aided by connections offered by professors, classmates, and alumni. Networking at events is also an excellent way to discover opportunities. Shows, displays, and contests in school, out of school, in the summer, or through social media can help you get noticed.

Throughout your varied experiences, you will meet other illustrators who may recommend you or inform you about open positions or contract opportunities, even some that are not publicly announced. In addition, many schools have a culminating event where you can put your best foot forward and showcase your work. Exposure to industry professionals can open new doors while interacting with people online or in-person will allow you to maintain those connections.

Autonomy and freedom to choose the jobs you take by venturing out on your own may seem alluring, but freelancing may result in uncertainty or even career limitations. As a result, companies often choose seasoned professionals with work experience in other firms. However, there are ways to mitigate against the lean times of solo work. A few options include demonstrating mastery, producing amazing work, resolving client problems, aligning ideologies, and initially charging less. Despite challenges, put yourself out there.

You could wait for the phone to ring to be discovered. However, you should post regularly and be out and about for that to happen. Some individuals pine away, hoping to be selected and deciding which organization would be a perfect fit. Others decide that they only want to work at a specific firm or location. Still others determine that they will work for themselves and be their own boss. Yet, sometimes taking any position at the start is a steppingstone to your dream life, commitment to service, and opportunity to put your unique mark on society.

BOLD NETWORKING

Networking takes social skills and a bit of moxie. From elevator speeches and professional encounters to interviews and masterclasses, your job is to find a way to get your work in front of people and have them see your talent and your potential to contribute. You have something special and fresh ideas. Finally, there is a professional entity that will welcome your style, ingenuity, discipline, and impact.

How can you be recognized? Meet people; hand out your resume; give them your business card; ask for their business card; follow up; ask if you can call or meet them, even when approaching these professionals may seem uncomfortable. Stay in touch with people you meet, even if it is just happenstance or serendipity. Keep a log with each person's phone, e-mail, identifying information, and both date and location where you met. You never know when you will need it.

If you meet people professionally at a masterclass or workshop, even if you do not exchange information, you will recognize them at a later date. They may recognize you in a future event too. Keep training. You should always seek ways to improve, irrespective of your experience. Lifelong learning improves your ability to maintain up-to-date skills and transition to new ventures. The outside world's perspective changes more quickly with social media's instant influences.

Though you should not take workshops just for the sake of meeting people, when you attend, be present in your quest to lead, serve, and envision. If your focus is not on your improvement or development, you may appear insincere in your intentions. However, workshops, conferences, and contests can allow others to see your purpose, vision, and talent.

Big-ticket training does not always mean better trainers or opportunities. Find time to visit museums, survey your surroundings, and notice cultural changes. While gathering new thoughts, remember humility and open-mindedness go a long way. Defer to the wise and listen. There is much you can learn.

STAY IN TOUCH

Do not annoy busy people, but you can keep in touch every couple of months. Communicating more frequently is overwhelming. However, life is long. People who grow with their craft transition fluidly through life's career phases. In illustration and comic book design, contacts are essential in all phases of your career. Also, do not be surprised. Many go-getters seeking to gain a coveted contract do the following:

1. Speak at Chamber of Commerce meetings.
2. Attend art, design, and software trade shows.
3. Gain a following on Instagram and Pinterest.
4. Write a newsletter and publish it on LinkedIn and other sources.
5. Link your work to Facebook, Twitter, Instagram, Pinterest, and other social media.
6. Enter in design contests.
7. Join professional associations.
8. Attend social gatherings of potential customers.
9. Keep in touch with your professors.
10. Stay involved with your alumni associations.

Friendships matter. Become lifelong colleagues by finding friends who share mutual interests and offer a sounding board or connections to new opportunities. People tend to stay in touch with "important" people. Note to self: Your contemporaries or peers are important people...although possibly not yet. As you form lists of contacts, you are likely to know these people throughout your career.

Be audacious while also being authentic. Networking can sometimes appear fake or forced as if you are going out on a hunt to find people for your own benefit. Worse, the act of networking can appear like stalking for those who incessantly attempt to connect.

The mental image of this type of 'networking' conjures the vision of people congregating at meetings. Friendships and the mutual support of allies can be enormously helpful, though 20,000 or even 200,000 followers on your website do not mean you are popular. However, you can have unexpected meaningful exchanges if you get out, meet people, and live life.

There are times when deeply moving, casual conversations in non-professional settings could also turn into connections. Do not lose touch with people or burn bridges along the way. This industry is not that big, especially whatever subspecialty you choose. You will continually see extraordinary talent. You never know. They may contact you to collaborate one day or meet for coffee at an event.

COLLEGE AND CAREER CENTERS

Although illustration programs often have internal connections to help you secure an internship or job, you might also speak to someone at your campus career center. They often have interesting and possibly different prospects you might not get elsewhere. In addition, there may be a specific career liaison for their art programs. Connect with them for help in your search process. Besides, you might want a related job that utilizes your creative, design, problem-solving, and presentation skills.

Companies that attend comic book shows often hire graduates whose energy, initiative, and cutting-edge knowledge are invaluable. Design, camera, and software companies also appreciate those who can demonstrate their products. Adobe, for example, has more than 24,000 employees worldwide. These jobs may or may not be your dream job now, but you might be surprised where the position may lead you, and sometimes you just need employment to earn money and get yourself on your feet.

Career center coordinators often have excellent ideas of alternative options you may have never considered. Furthermore, they can assist you with creating a professional resume and cover letters for specific industries that are different from the ones you have for illustration and comic book design.

They may also connect you with past graduates in the industry who make excellent connections. Some of them may have been in your program and have been through the ropes, know a few people, and may be able to get you an interview or invite you to an industry event. Any contact may help you get your foot in the door or find a job to make money in the meantime.

LINKEDIN

LinkedIn is especially helpful for career searches. You can find numerous influential contacts on LinkedIn. After interviews or events, connect with each person you met on LinkedIn. Keep a contact list of individuals you get to know in your area of interest. Do not constantly try to connect with people you do not really know. However, if you have made the connection, occasionally keep in touch.

While some LinkedIn message boxes may be full and you may not get a reply, you can try. Some people have tens of thousands of LinkedIn followers. I have about 20,000 'contacts', which does not necessarily mean that I am important. Remember that a paycheck or lots of friends does not make you more worthy or successful. Worth and value emanate from within your heart. Occasionally, you hit on a lucky break. Though I do not have time to communicate with everyone, I have connected with some of my most inspiring authors, advisors, and intellectual leaders through LinkedIn.

FINALLY

Most people are willing to help you. Five percent will not. Thus, you have a 19 out of 20 chance of interacting with decent people who have the time and will give you advice. Don't lose faith in humanity just because you run into a few people who are too busy to stop for you or are too self-absorbed that they cannot answer your question.

Remember that talent is only the beginning. You need to sell yourself. As you organize your goals and responsibilities, remember to think one step ahead of where you want to be by making a game plan. Since actions speak louder than words, take action without complaining and spread kindness along the way. Burned bridges are tough to reconstruct.

Honesty and trustworthiness are worth more than any physical object. Earn this by working hard, being efficient, and telling the truth. Professionalism in your words and deeds is essential. Put away all distractions and focus on your tasks.

Texts and social media take a surprising amount of time. Every action you take is a steppingstone to your future. Discipline is achieved by creating a goal and making it happen.

A nice note, card, or gift reminds people you are thinking about them, even when you are incredibly busy. Good friends who have your best interest may know doors that are not yet open for you. Keep in touch with them.

So, go on a walk, meet people, and live fully. Serendipity happens when you live life. However, your education is immensely valuable. Success happens when preparation meets opportunity. Thus, preparation is the best way to generate luck. Finally, even the most disciplined person can be lazy or inefficient. Fight this. Stay active. Make your life happen for you. Here are a few things to remember as you go out to pursue your dreams.

- Work ethic is everything.
- Excellence is expected.
- Learn what you do not know on your own time.
- Come to work prepared.
- Take constructive criticism well.
- Be respectful and courteous.
- Keep your cool under pressure.
- Avoid being timid.
- Stay on task.
- Come early.
- Stay late.
- Take your work seriously.
- Do more than expected.
- Be humble and thoughtful.
- Read your e-mail/texts after hours in case something is important.
- Ask questions. No question is too stupid.
- The only stupid question is the one that is never asked.
- Maintain a clean workspace.
- Dress and act professionally.
- Don't gossip or complain.
- Play when you are done.
- Study hard, play hard – in that order.
- Avoid frustrating your phenomenally busy supervisor.
- Be straightforward, and don't beat around the bush.

You've Got This!

4
Regions

49
Programs

COLLEGE PROFILES AND REQUIREMENTS

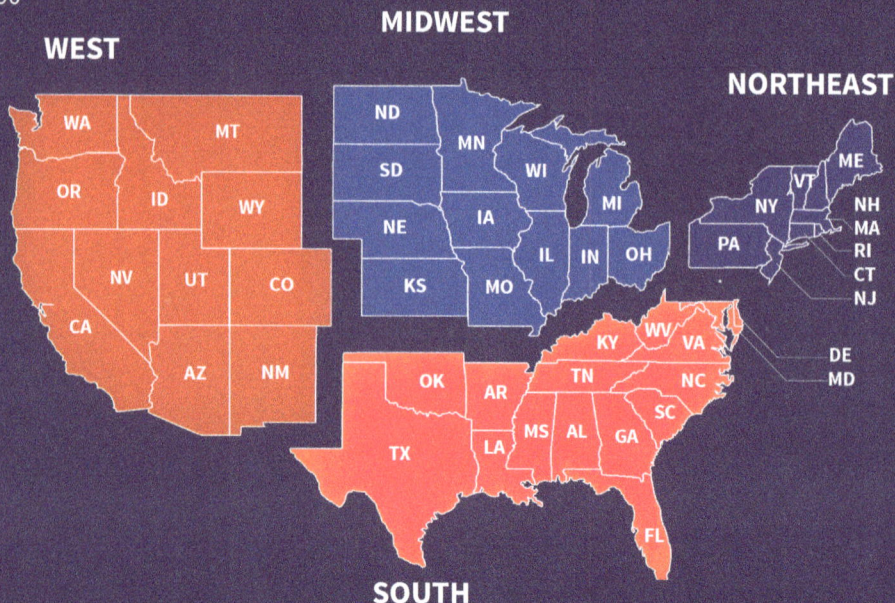

WEST

MIDWEST

NORTHEAST

SOUTH

PROGRAMS BY REGION
U.S. CENSUS BUREAU CLASSIFICATIONS

REGION 1 – NORTHEAST

Connecticut, Maine, Massachusetts, New Hampshire, New Jersey, New York, Pennsylvania, Rhode Island, and Vermont

REGION 2 – MIDWEST

Illinois, Indiana, Iowa, Kansas, Michigan, Minnesota, Missouri, Nebraska, North Dakota, Ohio, South Dakota, and Wisconsin

REGION 3 – SOUTH

Alabama, Arkansas, Delaware, District of Columbia, Florida, Georgia, Kentucky, Louisiana, Maryland, Mississippi, North Carolina, Oklahoma, South Carolina, Tennessee, Texas, Virginia, and West Virginia

REGION 4 – WEST

Alaska, Arizona, California, Colorado, Hawaii, Idaho, Montana, Nevada, New Mexico, Oregon, Utah, Washington, and Wyoming

LIST OF ILLUSTRATION & COMIC ART PROGRAMS

The 49 programs listed in the following pages include profiles of the top undergraduate illustration and comic art programs as of April 2022 along with additional college programs that offer closely related degrees. Many students interested in illustration and comic art are often also interested in drawing, painting, 3D design, graphic art, animation, and film, those schools are profiled in other books, though some lists are provided in the back.

Majoring in illustration and comic art is not for everyone. Although immensely rewarding, success requires initiative. Some students dual major for greater flexibility. In college, students discover their priorities, commitments, and perseverance. A few choose an alternative path somewhere down the road.

Thus, this book provides you with lists for other areas of art programs so you can explore those options. Keep the book handy. Even after you begin college, you may find that the summer and alternative college programs are helpful.

Creating lists is often tedious and cumbersome. These lists were gathered to help you with this task.

Descriptions of the college programs, tuition, requirements, and deadlines are accurate as of April 2022. However, the requirements may have changed by the time you purchase this book. Nevertheless, this information is a great place to start!

Note: To simplify the text and fit information into the charts and descriptions, abbreviations were used as well as shortened sentences and acronyms.

CONNECTICUT

MAINE

MASSACHUSETTS

NEW HAMPSHIRE

NEW JERSEY

NEW YORK

PENNSYLVANIA

RHODE ISLAND

VERMONT

CHAPTER 11

REGION ONE

NORTHEAST

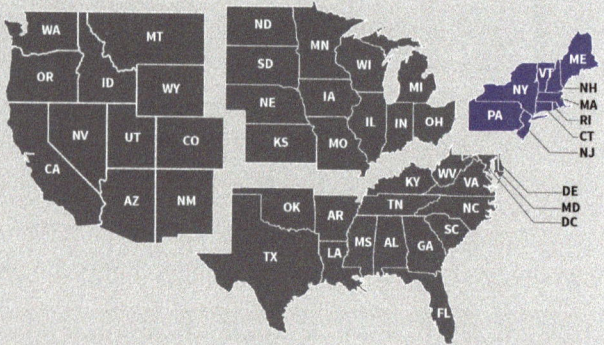

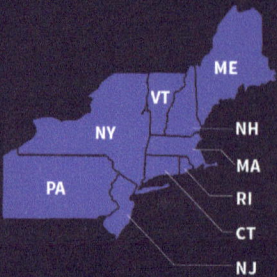

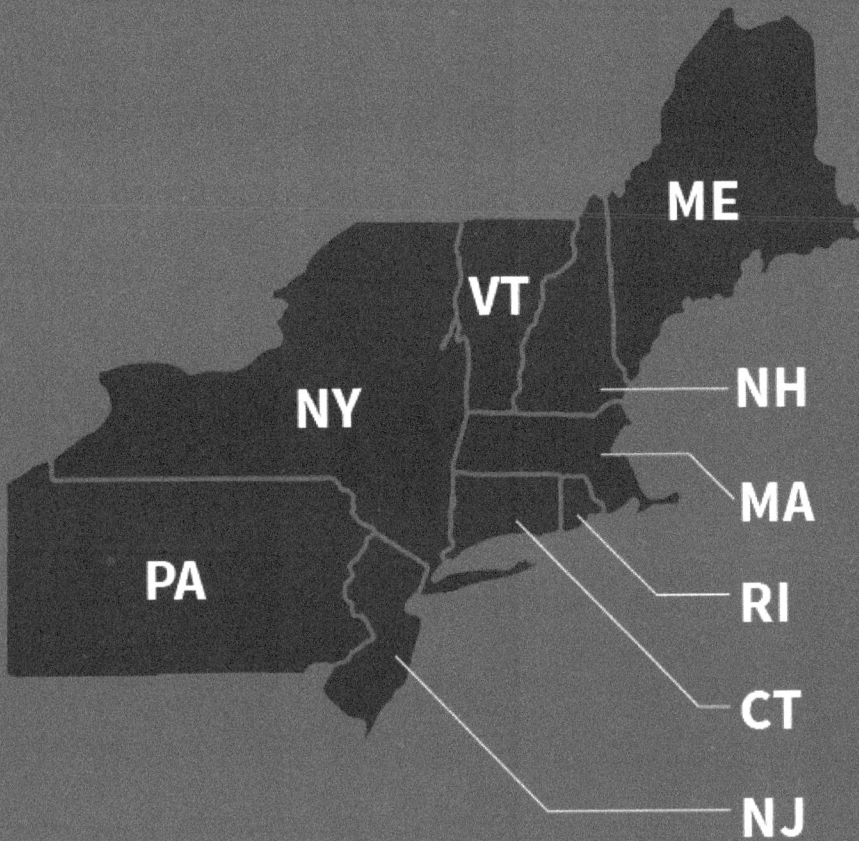

13 Programs | 9 States

School	Avg. GPA, SAT Evidence-Based Reading Writing (ERW), SAT Math (M), and ACT Composite (C) Early Decision (ED): Yes/No	Admission Statistics	Program(s)	Portfolio Required (req.)
University of Connecticut (UConn) 802 Bolton Rd., Unit-1127, Storrs, CT 06269	GPA: N/A SAT (ERW): 580-680 SAT (M): 590-710 ACT (C): 27-32 ED: No	Overall College Admit Rate: 56% Undergrad Enrollment: 18,917 Total Enrollment: 27,215	BFA Art & Design, concentration: Illustration/Animation	Portfolio req.
University of Hartford - Hartt School 200 Bloomfield Avenue, West Hartford, CT 06117	GPA: N/A SAT (ERW): 510-610 SAT (M): 510-600 ACT (C): 22-29 ED: No	Overall College Admit Rate: 77% Undergrad Enrollment: 4,521 Total Enrollment: 6,493	BFA Illustration	Portfolio req.
Maine College of Art & Design 522 Congress St., Portland, ME 04101	GPA: N/A SAT (ERW): N/A SAT (M): N/A ACT (C): N/A *Test-optional ED: No	Admit Rate: 70% Undergrad Enrollment: 380 Total Enrollment: 435	BFA Illustration	Portfolio req.
Massachusetts College of Art & Design 621 Huntington Ave, Boston, MA 02115	GPA: N/A SAT (ERW): N/A SAT (M): N/A ACT (C): N/A *Test-optional ED: No	Admit Rate: 70% Undergrad Enrollment: 1,770 Total Enrollment: 1,894	BFA Illustration	Portfolio req.

School	Avg. GPA, SAT Evidence-Based Reading Writing (ERW), SAT Math (M), and ACT Composite (C) Early Decision (ED): Yes/No	Admission Statistics	Program(s)	Portfolio Required (req.)
Fashion Institute of Technology (FIT) 227 West 27th Street, New York City, NY 10001	GPA: N/A SAT (ERW): N/A SAT (M): N/A ACT (C): N/A *FIT is test optional. ED: No	Admit Rate: 59% Undergrad Enrollment: 7,959 Total Enrollment: 8,191	BFA Illustration	Portfolio req.
Parsons - The New School 66 Fifth Avenue, New York, NY 10011	GPA: N/A SAT (ERW): 580-680 SAT (M): 560-680 ACT (C): 26-30 ED: No	Admit Rate: 69% Undergrad Enrollment: 6,399 Total Enrollment: 9,047	BFA Illustration	Portfolio req.
Pratt Institute 200 Willoughby Avenue, Brooklyn, NY 11205	GPA: 3.82 SAT (ERW): 570-660 SAT (M): 550-680 ACT (C): 25-30 ED: No	Admit Rate: 66% Undergrad Enrollment: 3,122 Total Enrollment: 4,353	BFA Communications Design, emphasis: Illustration	Portfolio req.
Rochester Institute of Technology 1 Lomb Memorial Dr, Rochester, NY 14623	GPA: 3.7 SAT (ERW): 600-690 SAT (M): 620-730 ACT (C): 28-33 ED: No	Overall College Admit Rate: 74% Undergrad Enrollment: 13,142 Total Enrollment: 16,158	BFA Illustration BFA Medical Illustration	Portfolio req.

NORTHEAST

School	Avg. GPA, SAT Evidence-Based Reading Writing (ERW), SAT Math (M), and ACT Composite (C) Early Decision (ED): Yes/No	Admission Statistics	Program(s)	Portfolio Required (req.)
School of Visual Arts (SVA) 209 East 23rd Street, New York, NY 10010	GPA: 3.91 SAT (ERW): 545-650 SAT (M): 530-680 ACT (C): 23-27 ED: No	Overall College Admit Rate: 72% Undergrad Enrollment: 3,192 Total Enrollment: 3,692	BFA Illustration	Portfolio req.
Syracuse University 401 University Place, Syracuse, NY 13244-2130	GPA: 3.67 SAT (ERW): N/A SAT (M): N/A ACT (C): N/A ED: Yes	Overall College Admit Rate: 69% Undergrad Enrollment: 14,479 Total Enrollment: 21,322	BFA Illustration	Portfolio req.
Pennsylvania Academy of Fine Arts (PAFA) 118-128 North Broad Street, Philadelphia, PA 19102	GPA: N/A SAT (ERW): N/A* SAT (M): N/A* ACT (C): N/A* *Test-optional ED: No	Overall College Admit Rate: 88% Undergrad Enrollment: 135 Total Enrollment: 188	BFA Illustration	Portfolio req.
University of the Arts 320 S. Broad Street, Philadelphia, PA 19102	GPA: N/A SAT (ERW): N/A* SAT (M): N/A* ACT (C): N/A* *Test-optional ED: No	Overall College Admit Rate: 76% Undergrad Enrollment: 1,380 Total Enrollment: 1,530	BFA Illustration	Portfolio req.

School	Avg. GPA, SAT Evidence-Based Reading Writing (ERW), SAT Math (M), and ACT Composite (C) Early Decision (ED): Yes/No	Admission Statistics	Program(s)	Portfolio Required (req.)
Rhode Island School of Design (RISD) 2 College St, Providence, RI 02903	GPA: N/A SAT (ERW): 610-700 SAT (M): 640-770 ACT (C): 27-32 ED: Yes	Admit Rate: 27% Undergrad Enrollment: 1,736 Total Enrollment: 2,227	BFA Illustration	Portfolio req.

NORTHEAST

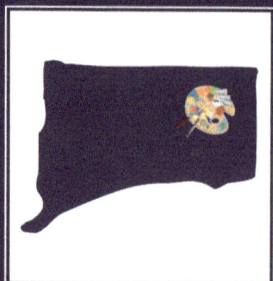

CONNECTICUT

MAINE

MASSACHUSETTS

NEW HAMPSHIRE

NEW JERSEY

NEW YORK

PENNSYLVANIA

RHODE ISLAND

VERMONT

UNIVERSITY OF CONNECTICUT (UCONN)

Address: 802 Bolton Rd., Unit-1127, Storrs, CT 06269
Website: *https://art.uconn.edu/illustration-animation/*
Contact: *https://admissions.uconn.edu/*
Phone: (860) 486-3137
Email: beahusky@uconn.edu

COST OF ATTENDANCE:

In-State Tuition & Fees: $15,030 | **Additional Expenses:** $16,752
Total: $31,782

New England Tuition & Fees: $24,048 | **Additional Expenses:** $16,752
Total: $40,800

Out-of-State Tuition & Fees: $37,698 | **Additional Expenses:** $16,752
Total: $54,450

Financial Aid: https://financialaid.uconn.edu/

ADDITIONAL INFORMATION:

Available Degree(s)

- BFA Art & Design, concentration: Illustration/Animation

Portfolio Requirement

Portfolios are required for incoming students. Submit 15-20 of your best works.

Scholarships Offered

First-year applicants are automatically considered for most merit scholarships offered at the University of Connecticut. The Nutmeg and Day of Pride scholarships require a school counselor nomination.

Special Opportunities

According to Uconn, the Illustration/Animation concentration educates students on visual storytelling and stresses the "creation of images that expand a text". Students gain technical and professional skills. Projects explore analog and digital environments. Students learn about product design, comics, graphic novels, children's illustration, character design, and more.

Notable Alumni

Scott DaRos, Alexis DePrey, and Rick Sternbach

UNIVERSITY OF HARTFORD

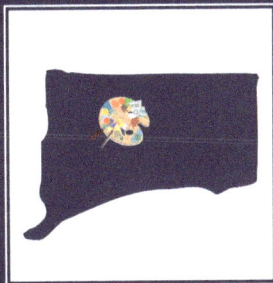

Address: 200 Bloomfield Avenue, West Hartford, CT 06117
Website: *https://www.hartford.edu/academics/schools-colleges/art/academics/undergraduate/illustration.aspx#*
Contact: *https://www.hartford.edu/contact.aspx*
Phone: (860) 768-4100
Email: uofhart@hartford.edu

COST OF ATTENDANCE:

Tuition & Fees: $44,885 | **Additional Expenses:** $17,667
Total: $62,552

Financial Aid: https://www.hartford.edu/admission/financial-aid/default.aspx

ADDITIONAL INFORMATION:

Available Degree(s)

- BFA Illustration

Portfolio Requirement

Portfolios are required for incoming students. Submit 10-15 of your best works from the past two years. All media accepted.

Scholarships Offered

Students are automatically considered for merit-based and need-based scholarships when they apply to the University of Hartford.

Special Opportunities

In Hartford's Illustration program, students learn professional standards/skills, technical expertise, and how to merge a client's needs with the artist's personal style. Students may take electives in portfolio prep, advertising, editorial, book preparation, and more.

Notable Alumni

Cindy Lau, Nick Napoletano, and Jackie Roche

CONNECTICUT

MAINE

MASSACHUSETTS

NEW HAMPSHIRE

NEW JERSEY

NEW YORK

PENNSYLVANIA

RHODE ISLAND

VERMONT

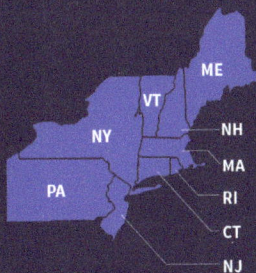

NORTHEAST

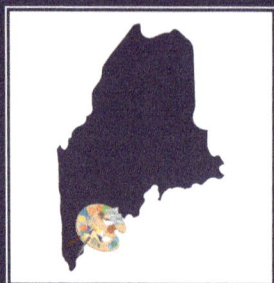

CONNECTICUT

MAINE

MASSACHUSETTS

NEW HAMPSHIRE

NEW JERSEY

NEW YORK

PENNSYLVANIA

RHODE ISLAND

VERMONT

MAINE COLLEGE OF ART & DESIGN

Address: 522 Congress St., Portland, ME 04101
Website: *https://www.meca.edu/academics/undergraduate/bfa-majors/illustration/*
Contact: *https://www.meca.edu/admissions/meet-the-staff/*
Phone: (800) 699-1509
Email: admissions@meca.edu

COST OF ATTENDANCE:

Tuition & Fees: $40,601 | **Additional Expenses:** $20,515
Total: $61,116

Financial Aid: https://www.meca.edu/admissions/undergraduate/tuition-financial-aid/types-of-aid/

ADDITIONAL INFORMATION:

Available Degree(s)

- BFA Illustration

Portfolio Requirement

Portfolios are required for incoming students. Submit 15-20 of your best works within the past two years. Three of the pieces must be drawings from direct observation. Submit via SlideRoom.

Scholarships Offered

MECA&D holds a BFA Full Tuition Scholarship competition each year. To be considered for this scholarship, applicants need to submit their application by February 1st. Applicants are judged on their portfolio submission. Additionally, first-year merit-based scholarships are available, ranging from $10,000-$21,000 per year.

Special Opportunities

Illustration students study technical skills as well as history, theory, and professional practices. Students engage with professionals in the industry through studio visits, field trips, and portfolio reviews. All fourth year illustration majors must take Professional Studio, a course where they learn about business practices and how to network.

Notable Alumni

Alysa Avery, Alexandra Cecililio, Thomas Dowling, Bridget Dunigan, Jada Fitch, Erica Gammon, Juliana Lawrence, Mary Anne Lloyd, Michaela Lyons, Alison McCahon, Garvin Morris, Cynthia Norrie, Zoe Reifsnyder, Briana Ring, Joe Rosshirt, Elise Smorczewski, Lori Stebbins, Anne Townsend, Peter Wallis, Bret Weese, and Phoenix Zoellick

MASSACHUSETTS COLLEGE OF ART & DESIGN (MASSART)

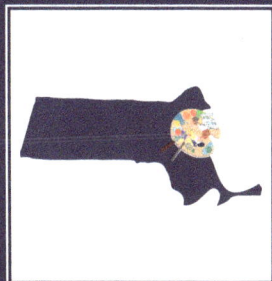

Address: 621 Huntington Ave, Boston, MA 02115
Website: *https://massart.edu/degree-programs/illustration-bfa*
Contact: *https://massart.edu/contactus*
Phone: (617) 879-7000
Email: admissions@massart.edu

COST OF ATTENDANCE:

In-State Tuition & Fees: $14,200 | **Additional Expenses:** $19,200
Total: $33,400

New England Resident: $31,800 | **Additional Expenses:** $19,200
Total: $51,000

Out-of-State Tuition & Fees: $39,800 | **Additional Expenses:** $19,200
Total: $59,000

Financial Aid: https://massart.edu/financial-aid

ADDITIONAL INFORMATION:

Available Degree(s)

- BFA Illustration

Portfolio Requirement

Portfolios are required for incoming students. Submit 15-20 examples of best and most recent work via the Common App. Applicants must not include artwork that copies another artist's work. Creative writing, screenplays, musical recordings, and theater performances are not allowed either.

Scholarships Offered

All eligible applicants are automatically considered for merit scholarships. To be considered, students need to demonstrate high academic achievement and showcase a strong portfolio. Out-of-state applicants may be eligible for the MassArt Merit Scholarship, the MassArt Transfer Merit Scholarship, or the Trustees Scholarship (covers all tuition and fees, renewable for four years). In-state applicants may be considered for the MassArt Merit Scholarship, the MassArt Transfer Merit Scholarship, and the Senator Paul E. Tsongas Scholarship (covers all tuition and fees for four years).

Special Opportunities

As stated by MassArt, a key tenet of the illustration program is being able to draw from observation. Students learn how to render images via various mediums. They learn how to use electronic media and how to weave different mediums with illustrated images to tell a story visually. The program culminates in a thesis project that is developed into a portfolio that is used to apply for jobs.

Notable Alumni

Calvin Burnett, Ben Edlund, Ed Emberly, Ben Jones, Poli Marichal, Toni Millionaire, and N.C. Wyeth

CONNECTICUT

MAINE

MASSACHUSETTS

NEW HAMPSHIRE

NEW JERSEY

NEW YORK

PENNSYLVANIA

RHODE ISLAND

VERMONT

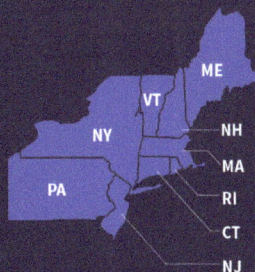

NORTHEAST

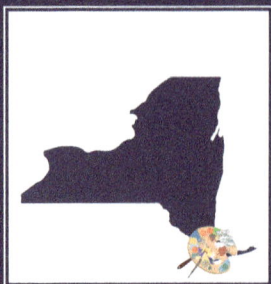

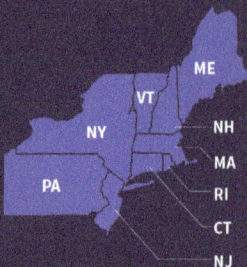

FASHION INSTITUTE OF TECHNOLOGY (FIT)

Address: 227 West 27th Street, New York City, NY 10001
Website: *https://www.fitnyc.edu/academics/academic-divisions/art-and-design/illustration/index.php*
Contact: *http://www.fitnyc.edu/about/contact/index.php*
Phone: (212) 217-3760
Email: fitinfo@fitnyc.edu

COST OF ATTENDANCE:

In-State Tuition & Fees: $7,920 | **Additional Expenses:** $18,556
Total: $26,476

Out-of-State Tuition & Fees: $22,242 | **Additional Expenses:** $18,556
Total: $40,798

Financial Aid: https://www.fitnyc.edu/admissions/costs/financial-aid/index.php

ADDITIONAL INFORMATION:

Available Degree(s)

- AAS Illustration
- BFA Illustration

Portfolio Requirement

Incoming first-year students must apply for the AAS Illustration. Once they earn the AAS, they may apply for the BFA in Illustration. Portfolios are required for incoming students. Submit 2 short essays and 14-20 works via SlideRoom.

Scholarships Offered

FIT scholarships are donor scholarships typically gifted to students with high financial need. The average award is $1,100.

Special Opportunities

FIT's illustration program integrates technical drawing skills with technology to create dynamic images. Students develop their artistic style while producing professional-quality work. A high-profile outdoor mural project is available annually for students to showcase their work to the public.

Notable Alumni

Timothy D. Bellavia and Antonio Lopez

CONNECTICUT

MAINE

MASSACHUSETTS

NEW HAMPSHIRE

NEW JERSEY

NEW YORK

PENNSYLVANIA

RHODE ISLAND

VERMONT

ME
VT
NY
NH
MA
RI
PA
CT
NJ

PARSONS - THE NEW SCHOOL

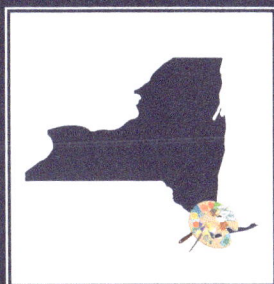

Address: 66 Fifth Avenue, New York, NY 10011
Website: *https://www.newschool.edu/parsons/bfa-illustration/*
Contact: *https://www.newschool.edu/parsons/contact/*
Phone: (212) 229-8900
Email: thinkparsons@newschool.edu

COST OF ATTENDANCE:

Tuition & Fees: $51,722 | **Additional Expenses:** N/A
Total: $51,722

Financial Aid: https://www.newschool.edu/financial-aid/

ADDITIONAL INFORMATION:

Available Degree(s)

- BFA Illustration

Portfolio Requirement

Portfolios are required for incoming students. Applicants must complete the Parsons Challenge, a new visual work inspired by a theme set by the university. Applicants must also submit 8-12 works. Submit via SlideRoom.

Scholarships Offered

The New School offers merit-based and need-based aid to students. Students are automatically considered for merit-based scholarships. These are based on the strength of the application and portfolio. Need-based aid is available to students who are eligible and submit the FAFSA.

Special Opportunities

Parsons offers a minor in Comics and Graphic Narrative. Illustration students apply their learning to professional internships during their studies. In the past, students have interned at Nickelodeon, Toon Books, the New York Times, and more.

Notable Alumni

George Bates, Ingo Fast, AJ Fosik, Leah Hayes, David Horvath, Sun-Min Kim, Adam McCauley, Motomichi Nakamura, Isabel Samaras, Peter de Seve, Robert Sikoryak, and Aaron Stewart

CONNECTICUT

MAINE

MASSACHUSETTS

NEW HAMPSHIRE

NEW JERSEY

NEW YORK

PENNSYLVANIA

RHODE ISLAND

VERMONT

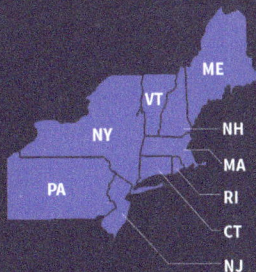

NORTHEAST

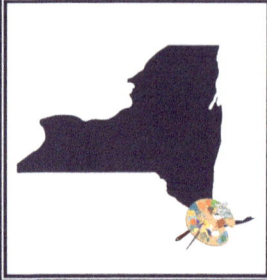

CONNECTICUT

MAINE

MASSACHUSETTS

NEW HAMPSHIRE

NEW JERSEY

NEW YORK

PENNSYLVANIA

RHODE ISLAND

VERMONT

PRATT INSTITUTE

Address: 200 Willoughby Avenue, Brooklyn, NY 11205
Website: *https://catalog.pratt.edu/undergraduate/design/
communications-design/communications-design-bfa-illustration/*
Contact: *https://www.pratt.edu/academics/school-of-design/
undergraduate-school-of-design/fashion/fashion-department-
contact/*
Phone: (718) 636-3600
Email: admissions@pratt.edu

COST OF ATTENDANCE:

Tuition & Fees: $53,566 | **Additional Expenses:** $19,824
Total: $73,390

Financial Aid: https://www.pratt.edu/admissions/financing-your-
education/financing-undergraduate/

ADDITIONAL INFORMATION:

Available Degree(s)

- BFA Communications Design, emphasis: Illustration

Portfolio Requirement

Portfolios are required for incoming students. Submit via Slideroom.

Scholarships Offered

Pratt offers merit-based and endowed scholarships in addition
to need-based grants. Furthermore, there are merit-based
scholarships available to international students as well. The
Presidential Merit-Based Scholarships are available to all Pratt
students in varied award amounts.

Special Opportunities

Students in the illustration emphasis take coursework such as
advanced storytelling, sociopolitical commentary, and authorship.
Students are encouraged to experiment across mediums,
technologies, and platforms. Electives include graphic novels, 3D
modeling, children's books, concept art, and more.

Notable Alumni

Marshall Arisman, Kenneth Bald, Joseph Barbera, C.C. Beall, Dave
Berg, Bernard Chang, Daniel Clowes, Frances W. Delehanty, Gus
Edson, Tomie dePaola, Jules Feiffer, Bill Griffith, Cheryl Hanna, Joe
Harris, Candy Jernigan, Jack Kirby, Albert Konetzni, Morton Meskin,
Jacqui Morgan, Kadir Nelson, Martin Nodell, Roberto Parada,
Mike Roy, Robert Sabuda, Bernard Safran, Sam Savitt, Gordon A.
Sheehan, Joseph A. Smith, Pamela Colman Smith, Kevin Stanton,
Leonard Starr, Samm Schwartz, Cindy Szekeres, and Chris Tsirgiotis

ROCHESTER INSTITUTE OF TECHNOLOGY

Address: 209 East 23rd Street, New York, NY 10010
Website: *https://www.rit.edu/study/illustration-bfa*
Contact: *https://www.rit.edu/admissions/contacts*
Phone: (585) 475-6631
Email: admissions@rit.edu

COST OF ATTENDANCE:

Tuition & Fees: $54,058 | **Additional Expenses:** $18,296
Total: $72,354

Financial Aid: https://www.rit.edu/admissions/financial-aid

ADDITIONAL INFORMATION:

Available Degree(s)

- BFA Illustration
- BFA Medical Illustration

Portfolio Requirement

Portfolios are required for incoming students. Submit 10-20 works via Slideroom. At least three works must be drawings from direct observation. BFA Medical Illustration applicants must include at least 6 works of natural forms, such as the human figure, shells, bones, or plants from direct observation.

Scholarships Offered

All applicants are considered for merit-based scholarships upon submission of their application. No separate application is required. RIT also offers numerous merit-based and need-based scholarships for students from different backgrounds or different majors.

Special Opportunities

Coursework for Illustration students focuses on traditional drawing skills, digital techniques, conceptual skills, narrative storytelling approaches, and how to develop your personal style. Graduates go on to work in advertising, publishing, editorial, and gaming industries.

Notable Alumni

Brian Bram, Adam Kubert, Glynis Sweeny, and Eloise Wilkin

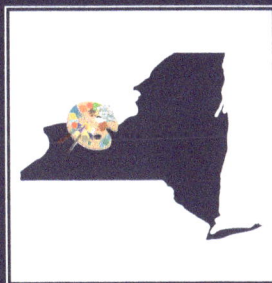

CONNECTICUT

MAINE

MASSACHUSETTS

NEW HAMPSHIRE

NEW JERSEY

NEW YORK

PENNSYLVANIA

RHODE ISLAND

VERMONT

NORTHEAST

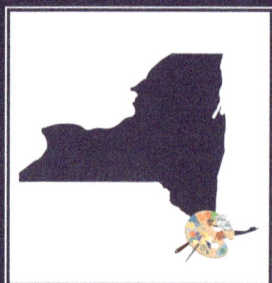

CONNECTICUT

MAINE

MASSACHUSETTS

NEW HAMPSHIRE

NEW JERSEY

NEW YORK

PENNSYLVANIA

RHODE ISLAND

VERMONT

SCHOOL OF VISUAL ARTS (SVA)

Address: 209 East 23rd Street, New York, NY 10010
Website: *https://sva.edu/academics/undergraduate/bfa-illustration*
Contact: *https://sva.edu/contact-and-map*
Phone: (212) 592- 2100
Email: admissions@sva.edu

COST OF ATTENDANCE:

Tuition & Fees: $49,750 | **Additional Expenses:** N/A
Total: $49,750

Financial Aid: https://sva.edu/admissions/financial-resources/
financial-aid

ADDITIONAL INFORMATION:

Available Degree(s)

- BFA Illustration
- BFA Cartooning

Portfolio Requirement

Portfolios are required for incoming students. Submit 15-20 works
via SlideRoom.

Scholarships Offered

The Silad H. Rhodes Scholarship is available to students of all
majors with an unlisted award amount. Students with a GPA of
3.0+ are eligible. First-time freshmen applicants must submit all
application materials by February to be considered. There is no
separate application.

Special Opportunities

In their junior year, illustration students complete their thesis
project. By the fourth year, students learn how to compile their
works into professional portfolios, ready for applications to
companies post-graduation. Electives include Motion Graphic
Techniques, Introduction to Stop Motion, Creating Unforgettable
Characters, and more.

Notable Alumni

Josh Adams, Sal Amendola, Ross Andru, Peter Bagge, Chris Batista,
Liz Berube, Gene Bilbrew, Ray Billingsley, Mark Bode, Federico
Castelluccio, Joey Cavalieri, R. Gregory Christie, Matt Davies, Paul
Davis, Steve Ditko, Mike Esposito, Tom Feelings, Bill Gallo, Robert
Gilbert, Stan Goldberg, Jordan Gorfinkel, Bo Hampton, Timer
Hanuka, Yumi Heo, John Holmstrom, Dick Hodgins, Jr., Jamal Igle,
Larry Ivie, Kaz, Ken Landgraf, Keith Harring, Patrick McDonnel, Tom
Moore, Molly Ostertag, Nate Powell, Joe Quesada, Khary Randolph,
Tim Sale, Alex Saviuk, Yuko Shimizu, Joe Sinnott, Eric Stanton,
James Sturm, Tony Tallarico, Mark Texeira, Herb Trimpe, Sara Varon,
John Verpoorten, Bob Wiacek, Wally Wood, and Madeline Zuluaga

SYRACUSE UNIVERSITY

Address: 202 Crouse College, Syracuse, NY 13244
Website: *https://vpa.syr.edu/academics/art/programs/illustration-bfa/*
Contact: *https://www.syracuse.edu/admissions/undergraduate/contact/*
Phone: (315) 443-2769
Email: admissu@syr.edu

COST OF ATTENDANCE:

Tuition & Fees: $57,591 | **Additional Expenses:** $44,448.8
Total: $80,039.80

Financial Aid: https://www.syracuse.edu/admissions/cost-and-aid/

ADDITIONAL INFORMATION:

Available Degree(s)

- BFA Illustration

Portfolio Requirement

Portfolios are required for incoming students. Submit 12-20 works that emphasize your strengths and a variety of approaches. Syracuse University strongly encourages applicants to submit at least 6 drawings from observation.

Scholarships Offered

Syracuse University offers various merit-based and need-based scholarships and grants. The 1870 Scholarship covers full tuition for the full length of the undergraduate program. Artistic Scholarships are awarded to students based on talent and a maintained cumulative GPA of 2.75+.

Special Opportunities

Illustration students study traditional, digital, and alternative techniques. Students may focus on industry specialities, including Visual Development, Editorial, Sequential, and Product. Syracuse hosts guest lecturers, workshops, and trips to New York City. Illustration majors are encouraged to study abroad, and most travel to the Syracuse University campus in Florence, Italy or complete a two-week immersion in Los Angeles.

Notable Alumni

Robb Armstrong, Brad Anderson, Jim Burke, Robert Mankoff, Scott McCloud, and Jack Tippit

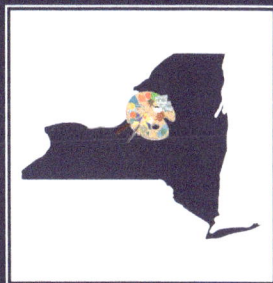

CONNECTICUT

MAINE

MASSACHUSETTS

NEW HAMPSHIRE

NEW JERSEY

NEW YORK

PENNSYLVANIA

RHODE ISLAND

VERMONT

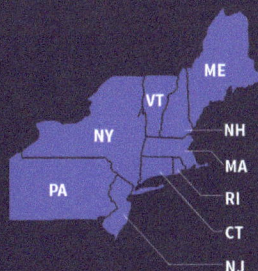

NORTHEAST

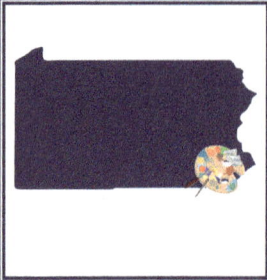

CONNECTICUT

MAINE

MASSACHUSETTS

NEW HAMPSHIRE

NEW JERSEY

NEW YORK

PENNSYLVANIA

RHODE ISLAND

VERMONT

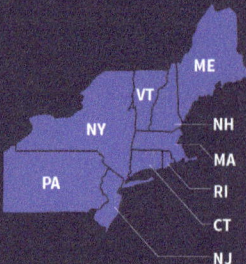

PENNSYLVANIA ACADEMY OF FINE ARTS (PAFA)

Address: 118-128 North Broad Street, Philadelphia, PA 19102
Website: *https://www.pafa.org/school/academics/areas-study-departments/illustration*
Contact: *https://www.pafa.org/about*
Phone: (215) 972-7600
Email: info@pafa.org

COST OF ATTENDANCE:

Tuition & Fees: $36,058 | **Additional Expenses:** $23,204
Total: $59,262

Financial Aid: https://www.pafa.org/school/admissions/financing-your-education/types-financial-aid

ADDITIONAL INFORMATION:

Available Degree(s)

- BFA Illustration

Portfolio Requirement

Portfolios are required for incoming students. Submit 12-15 images via Slideroom.

Scholarships Offered

According to PAFA, 100% of their students receive merit scholarships. The average award is $19,722. Merit-based and need-based aid is available to all students.

Special Opportunities

This program is a unique, joint BFA degree between PAFA and UPenn. To apply to the joint program, applicants must first apply and enroll at PAFA. Accepted students then work with an advisor to complete their Penn application. Students may start coursework at Penn after successfully completing their first year at PAFA. If they do not get accepted to Penn, students may still complete their BFA at PAFA.

Notable Alumni

Michael Berenstain, Rutherford Boyd, Marie Bruner Haines, Charlotte Harding, George Matthews Harding, Ella Sophonisba Hergesheimer, Frances Tipton Hunter, Dorothy P. Lathrop, Herschel Levit, Leal Mack, and Henry Bainbridge McCarter

UNIVERSITY OF THE ARTS

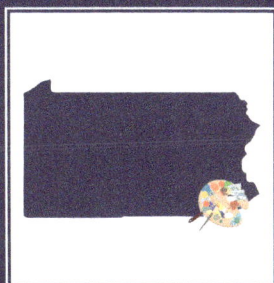

Address: 320 S. Broad Street, Philadelphia, PA 19102
Website: *https://www.uarts.edu/academics/illustration*
Contact: *https://www.uarts.edu/about/contact-us*
Phone: (215) 717-6049
Email: admissions@uarts.edu

COST OF ATTENDANCE:

Tuition & Fees: $48,350 | **Additional Expenses:** $20,600
Total: $68,950

Financial Aid: https://www.uarts.edu/tuition-and-financial-aid

ADDITIONAL INFORMATION:

Available Degree(s)

- BFA Illustration

Portfolio Requirement

Portfolios are required for incoming students. Submit 15-20 works from the past two years.

Scholarships Offered

Various named scholarships are available to all students for varied award amounts. Some scholarships are available to all University of the Arts students, such as the W.W. Smith Scholarship, the James M. Cresson, Scholarship, the Arnold A. Bayard Scholarship, and more.

Special Opportunities

Illustration students share studio spaces with students in Animation, Fine Arts, Graphic Design, Interaction Design, and Product Design. This allows for a supportive environment and a multidisciplinary exposure to various mediums and art forms. Illustration students utilize the Cintiq Lab, as well as tools such as laser cutters and 3D printers. Students receive training in anatomy, typography, traditional painting methods, Adobe Creative Suite, and more.

Notable Alumni

Richard Amsel, Bascove, Jan Berenstain, Stan Berenstain, Aliki Brandenberg, Irv Docktor, Roger Hane, Frances Tipton Hunter, Harold Knerr, James Paul Kocsis, Jacob Landau, Katherine Milhous, Brothers Quay, Charles Santore, and Cal Schenkel

CONNECTICUT

MAINE

MASSACHUSETTS

NEW HAMPSHIRE

NEW JERSEY

NEW YORK

PENNSYLVANIA

RHODE ISLAND

VERMONT

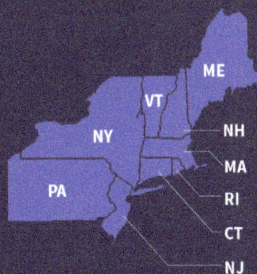

NORTHEAST

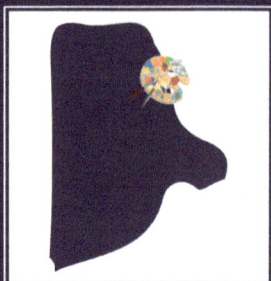

CONNECTICUT

MAINE

MASSACHUSETTS

NEW HAMPSHIRE

NEW JERSEY

NEW YORK

PENNSYLVANIA

RHODE ISLAND

VERMONT

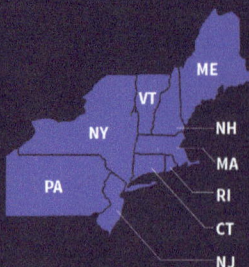

RHODE ISLAND SCHOOL OF DESIGN (RISD)

Address: 2 College St, Providence, RI 02903
Website: *https://www.risd.edu/academics/illustration/bachelors-program*
Contact: *https://www.risd.edu/academics/apparel-design/contact/*
Phone: (401) 454-6300
Email: admissions@risd.edu

COST OF ATTENDANCE:

Tuition & Fees: $55,220 | **Additional Expenses:** $22,060
Total: $77,280

Financial Aid: https://www.risd.edu/student-financial-services/undergraduate-aid/

ADDITIONAL INFORMATION:

Available Degree(s)

- BFA Illustration

Portfolio Requirement

Portfolios are required for incoming students. Submit 12-20 recent works via SlideRoom. Applicants are strongly encouraged to submit drawings from observation. Applicants must also complete The Assignment - a two-part portfolio requirement that involves a visual study based on a prompt.

Scholarships Offered

RISD scholarships are need-based. Students must submit a FAFSA application each year to be considered. RISD is also partnered with Scholarship Universe, a website that matches students with outside scholarships and keeps students on track with deadlines.

Special Opportunities

Illustration students may utilize any of the myriad of studio spaces and facilities available at RISD, including but not limited to Wacom drawing tablets, Litho presses, an etching press, a vacuum exposure unit, and software such as Dreamweaver, AfterEffects, Maya Autodesk, Premiere, and more.

Notable Alumni

Roz Chast, Elizabeth Updike Cobblah, Emiko Davies, Christopher Denise, Shepard Fairey, Jon Foster, Helen C. Frederick, Jessica Hess, Steven Kellogg, Jane Kim, Bryan Konietzko, Cynthia Lahti, Sonny Lieu, Sonny Liew, Grace Lin, Jason Lutes, Fred Lynch, David Macauley, David Mazzucchelli, Kelly Murphy, Antoine Revoy, Paolo Rivera, Julia Rothman, Brian Selznick, Mary Shaffer, Mark Shasha, Walt Simonson, Chris Van Allsburg, and David Wiesner

CHAPTER 12

REGION TWO

MIDWEST

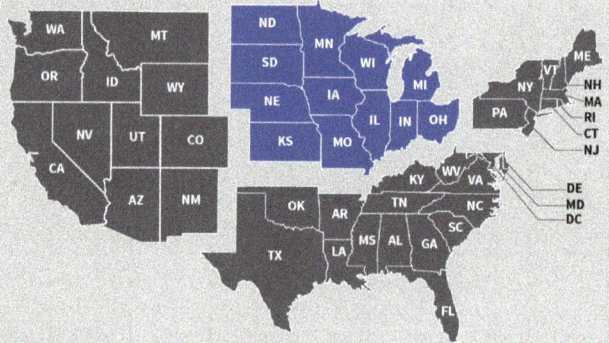

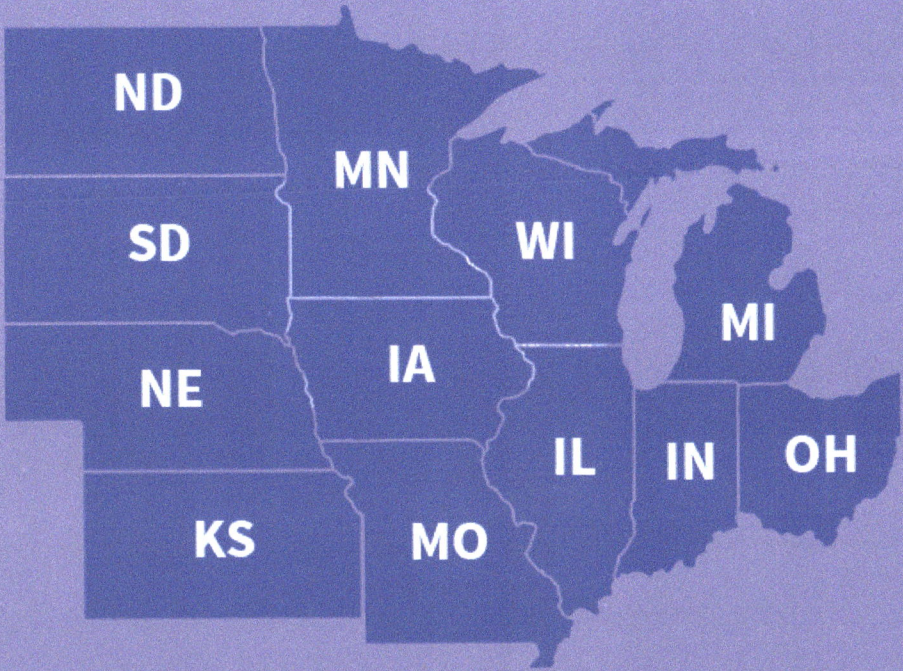

12 *Programs* | 12 *States*

1. *IL - Columbia College Chicago*
2. *IL - School of the Art Institute Chicago*
3. *IN - Purdue University*
4. *MI - College for Creative Studies*
5. *MI - Ferris State University*
6. *MN - Minneapolis College of Art & Design*
7. *KS - Kansas City Art Institute*
8. *MO - Washington University, St. Louis*
9. *OH - Art Academy of Cincinnati*
10. *OH - Cleveland Institute of Art*
11. *OH - Columbus College of Art & Design*
12. *WI - Milwaukee Institute of Art & Design*

ILLUSTRATION & COMIC ART PROGRAMS

School	Avg. GPA, SAT Evidence-Based Reading Writing (ERW), SAT Math (M), and ACT Composite (C) Early Decision (ED): Yes/No	Admission Statistics	Program(s)	Portfolio Required (req.)
Columbia College Chicago 600 S Michigan Ave, Chicago, IL 60605	GPA: N/A SAT (ERW): N/A* SAT (M): N/A* ACT (C): N/A* *Test-optional ED: Yes	Overall College Admit Rate: 90% Undergrad Enrollment: 6,542 Total Enrollment: 6,769	BFA Illustration BA Illustration	Portfolio req.
School of the Art Institute of Chicago (SAIC) 36 S. Wabash Ave., Chicago, IL 60603	GPA: N/A SAT (ERW): 560-660 SAT (M): 480-600 ACT (C): 22-25 ED: No	Admit Rate: 78% Undergrad Enrollment: 2,487 Total Enrollment: 3,132	BFA Studio	Portfolio req.
Purdue University Purdue University, West Lafayette, IN 47907	GPA: 3.67 SAT (ERW): 590-690 SAT (M): 600-740 ACT (C): 25-33 ED: No	Overall College Admit Rate: 67% Undergrad Enrollment: 34,920 Total Enrollment: 45,869	BFA Drawing & Illustration	Portfolio req.
College for Creative Studies 201 E. Kirby, Detroit, MI 48202	GPA: N/A SAT (ERW): N/A* SAT (M): N/A* ACT (C): N/A* *Not required nor accepted ED: No	Overall College Admit Rate: 55% Undergrad Enrollment: 1,462 Total Enrollment: 1,512	BFA Illustration	Portfolio req.

School	Avg. GPA, SAT Evidence-Based Reading Writing (ERW), SAT Math (M), and ACT Composite (C) Early Decision (ED): Yes/No	Admission Statistics	Program(s)	Portfolio Required (req.)
Ferris State University 1201 S. State Street, Big Rapids, MI, 49307	GPA: 3.32 SAT (ERW): 470-580 SAT (M): 470-580 ACT (C): 18-26 ED: No	Admit Rate: 82% Undergrad Enrollment: 9,929 Total Enrollment: 11,165	BFA Illustration BFA Life Sciences and Pre-Medical Illustration	Portfolio req.
Minneapolis College of Art & Design 2501 Stevens Avenue, Minneapolis, MN 55404	GPA: N/A SAT (ERW): N/A* SAT (M): N/A* ACT (C): N/A* *Test-optional ED: No	Overall College Admit Rate: 55% Undergrad Enrollment: 670 Total Enrollment: 760	BFA Illustration	Portfolio req.
Kansas City Art Institute 4415 Warwick Blvd., Kansas City, MO 64111	GPA: N/A SAT (ERW): N/A* SAT (M): N/A* ACT (C): N/A* *Test-optional ED: No	Overall College Admit Rate: 59% Undergrad Enrollment: 698 Total Enrollment: 698	BFA Illustration	Portfolio req.
Washington University in St. Louis 1 Brookings Dr, St. Louis, MO 63130	GPA: 4.21 SAT (ERW): 720-760 SAT (M): 760-800 ACT (C): 33-35 ED: Yes	Overall College Admit Rate: 16% Undergrad Enrollment: 7,653 Total Enrollment: 15,449	BFA Communication Design, emphasis: Illustration	Portfolio req.

MIDWEST

ILLUSTRATION & COMIC ART PROGRAMS

School	Avg. GPA, SAT Evidence-Based Reading Writing (ERW), SAT Math (M), and ACT Composite (C) Early Decision (ED): Yes/No	Admission Statistics	Program(s)	Portfolio Required (req.)
Art Academy of Cincinnati 1212 Jackson St, Cincinnati, OH 45202	GPA: N/A SAT (ERW): N/A* SAT (M): N/A* ACT (C): N/A* *Test-optional ED: No	Overall College Admit Rate: 31% Undergrad Enrollment: 227 Total Enrollment: 235	BFA Illustration	Portfolio req.
Cleveland Institute of Art 11610 Euclid Avenue, Cleveland, OH 44106	GPA: N/A SAT (ERW): 560-680 SAT (M): 510-620 ACT (C): 19-27 ED: No	Overall College Admit Rate: 67% Undergrad Enrollment: 599 Total Enrollment: 599	BFA Illustration	Portfolio req.
Columbus College of Art and Design 60 Cleveland Ave, Columbus, OH 43215	GPA: N/A SAT (ERW): N/A SAT (M): N/A ACT (C): N/A *Test-optional ED: No	Admit Rate: 92% Undergrad Enrollment: 982 Total Enrollment: 1,009	BFA Illustration BFA Comics & Narrative Practice	Portfolio req.
Milwaukee Institute of Art & Design 273 E Erie St, Milwaukee, WI 53202	GPA: N/A SAT (ERW): N/A* SAT (M): N/A* ACT (C): N/A* *Test-optional ED: No	Overall College Admit Rate: 62% Undergrad Enrollment: 925 Total Enrollment: 925	BFA Illustration	Portfolio req.

COLUMBIA COLLEGE CHICAGO

Address: 600 S. Michigan Avenue, Chicago, IL 60605
Website: *https://www.colum.edu/academics/programs/illustration*
Contact: *https://www.colum.edu/contact*
Phone: (312) 369-1000
Email: admissions@colum.edu

COST OF ATTENDANCE:

Tuition & Fees: $35,716 | **Additional Expenses:** $18,000
Total: $53,716

Financial Aid: https://www.colum.edu/columbia-central/where-to-start/index

ADDITIONAL INFORMATION:

Available Degree(s)

- BFA Illustration
- BA Illustration

Portfolio Requirement

Portfolios are required for the BFA program. They are optional for the BA. However, to be considered for the Faculty Recognition Award, a portfolio must be submitted. Submit 15-20 works in a variety of media.

Scholarships Offered

Students are automatically considered for renewable scholarships upon admission. For need-based scholarship, submit a FAFSA. For talent-based scholarships, submit an audition that demonstrates your best creative work. First-year, international students may be considered for talent-based scholarships.

Special Opportunities

Illustration students learn three commercial models within the field: freelance, institutional, and contract-based. They learn the technical and business skills necessary to gain employment post-graduation. Students often gain internships during their time at Columbia College Chicago.

Notable Alumni

David Alvarado, Ali Cantarella, Nick Drnaso, Erik Lundquist, Keara McGraw, Heidi Unkefer, and Julie Wilmore

ILLINOIS

INDIANA

IOWA

KANSAS

MICHIGAN

MINNESOTA

MISSOURI

NEBRASKA

NORTH DAKOTA

OHIO

SOUTH DAKOTA

WISCONSIN

SCHOOL OF THE ART INSTITUTE OF CHICAGO (SAIC)

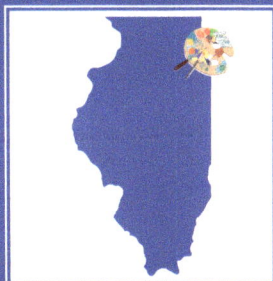

Address: 36 S. Wabash Ave., Chicago, IL 60603
Website: *https://www.saic.edu/academics/areas-of-study/illustration*
Contact: *https://www.saic.edu/contact/*
Phone: (312) 629-6101
Email: admiss@saic.edu

COST OF ATTENDANCE:

Tuition & Fees: $53,360 | **Additional Expenses:** $21,200
Total: $74,560

Financial Aid: https://www.saic.edu/financial-aid/

ADDITIONAL INFORMATION:

Available Degree(s)

- BFA Studio

Portfolio Requirement

Portfolios are required for incoming students. Submit 10-15 recent works.

Scholarships Offered

SAIC offers Presidential, Distinguished, Honors, Recognition, Incentive, and Enrichment scholarships at varied amounts. These merit scholarships are based on the student's portfolio and application materials. In addition, students who participated in certain art exhibitions or competitions may be eligible for the Competitive Excellence Award ($2000).

Need-based scholarships are also available. Some of these include the John and Mary E. Hoggins Scholarship for female SAIC students, the Roger Brown and George Veronda Scholarship, or the LeRoy Neiman Scholarship. Award amounts vary.

Special Opportunities

Studies at SAIC are interdisciplinary, where students do not declare a major and instead freely study among various areas of study. Students interested in illustration may be interested in coursework such as Beginning Fashion Illustration, Animation, Comics, or Typography.

Notable Alumni

Gene Ahern, Wilfrid Swancourt Bronson, Jeffrey Brown, Margaret Brundage, John Churchill Chase, Bradshaw Crandell, Walt Disney, Fred Ellis, Hal Foster, Edward Goery, Herblock, Ed Holland, J.C. Leyendecker, Shaw McCutcheon, Bill Mauldin, Chris Ware, and Gahan Wilson

ILLINOIS

INDIANA

IOWA

KANSAS

MICHIGAN

MINNESOTA

MISSOURI

NEBRASKA

NORTH DAKOTA

OHIO

SOUTH DAKOTA

WISCONSIN

MIDWEST

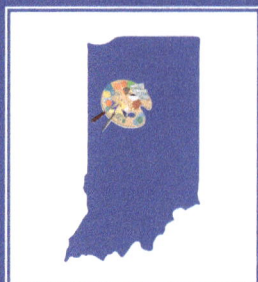

ILLINOIS

INDIANA

IOWA

KANSAS

MICHIGAN

MINNESOTA

MISSOURI

NEBRASKA

NORTH DAKOTA

OHIO

SOUTH DAKOTA

WISCONSIN

PURDUE UNIVERSITY

Address: Purdue University, West Lafayette, IN 47907
Website: *https://herron.iupui.edu/academics/udegrees/drawing-illustration/index.html*
Contact: *https://www.admissions.purdue.edu/contact/index.php*
Phone: (765) 494-4600
Email: admissions@purdue.edu

COST OF ATTENDANCE:

In-State Tuition & Fees: $10,052 | **Additional Expenses:** $12,820
Total: $22,872

Out-of-State Tuition & Fees: $28,854 | **Additional Expenses:** $12,820
Total: $41,674

Financial Aid: https://www.purdue.edu/dfa/

ADDITIONAL INFORMATION:

Available Degree(s)

- BFA Drawing & Illustration

Portfolio Requirement

Portfolios are required for incoming students. Submit recent works and an essay via SlideRoom.

Scholarships Offered

Purdue awards freshman scholarships based on academic merit as well as financial need. The Trustees Scholarship awards $10,000 per year to in-state students and $16,000 per year to out-of-state students. The Presidential Scholarship awards $4,000 per year to in-state students and $10,000 per year to out-of-state students.

Special Opportunities

Students in the Drawing & Illustration program explore approaches to storytelling in a variety of media, by experimenting with photography, sculpture, and printmaking. Students also have access to facilities such as light tables, digital labs, tablets, a shooting studio, an in-house gallery, and more. Drawing & Illustration students may also be interested in minoring in Book Arts or Graphic Design.

Notable Alumni

Robert K. Abbett, Harold Gray, John T. McCutcheon, and Mark O'Hare

COLLEGE FOR CREATIVE STUDIES

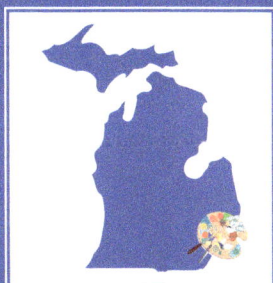

Address: 201 E. Kirby, Detroit, MI 48202
Website: *https://www.collegeforcreativestudies.edu/academics/ undergraduate-programs/illustration/*
Contact: *https://www.collegeforcreativestudies.edu/contact-us*
Phone: (313) 664-7425
Email: admissions@collegeforcreativestudies.edu

COST OF ATTENDANCE:

Tuition & Fees: $48,030 | **Additional Expenses:** $10,577
Total: $58,607

Financial Aid: https://www.collegeforcreativestudies. edu/admissions/scholarship-aid

ADDITIONAL INFORMATION:

Available Degree(s)

- BFA Illustration

Portfolio Requirement

Portfolios are required for incoming students. Submit at least 8 recent works via SlideRoom. Include at least 5 drawings from direct observation or imagination

Scholarships Offered

Applicants are automatically considered for CCS scholarships. CCS encourages students to explore outside scholarship opportunities.

Special Opportunities

Illustration students gain technical skills as well as professional skills at CCS. Business-centric courses prepare students for work outside of the classroom. Students may choose a pathway in the following areas: Visual Development, Publishing, Fashion, Lifestyle and Licensing, Comics & Sequential, or Gallery Artist. There is also an optional concentration in Entrepreneurial Studies.

Notable Alumni

Gary Brook, Katie Cook, Chris Houghton, Sydney G. James, Michael Maher, Kellye Purdue, and Ryan Savas

ILLINOIS

INDIANA

IOWA

KANSAS

MICHIGAN

MINNESOTA

MISSOURI

NEBRASKA

NORTH DAKOTA

OHIO

SOUTH DAKOTA

WISCONSIN

MIDWEST

ILLINOIS

INDIANA

IOWA

KANSAS

MICHIGAN

MINNESOTA

MISSOURI

NEBRASKA

NORTH DAKOTA

OHIO

SOUTH DAKOTA

WISCONSIN

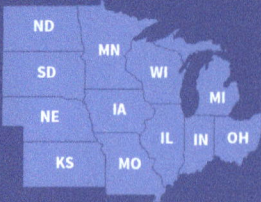

FERRIS STATE UNIVERSITY

Address: 1201 S. State Street, Big Rapids, MI, 49307
Website: *https://kcad.ferris.edu/programs/undergraduate/ illustration/index.html*
Contact: *https://www.ferris.edu/contact/homepage.htm*
Phone: (231) 591-2000
Email: https://www.ferris.edu/contact/homepage.htm

COST OF ATTENDANCE:

Tuition & Fees: $13,808 | **Additional Expenses:** $13,752
Total: $27,560

Financial Aid: https://www.ferris.edu/admissions/financialaid/index. html

ADDITIONAL INFORMATION:

Available Degree(s)

- BFA Illustration
- BFA Life Sciences and Pre-Medical Illustration

Portfolio Requirement

Portfolios are required for incoming students. Submit 8-10 recent works via SlideRoom.

Scholarships Offered

Ferris State offers various merit-based and need-based scholarships, ranging in value from $1,500 per year to $10,000 per year. Although Ferris State is a public university, they have eliminated out-of-state tuition. All U.S. citizens are charged the same.

Special Opportunities

Illustration students at Ferris State learn traditional and emerging media illustration techniques as well as visual storytelling. Students have access to the Dow Center FlexLab, the digital fabrication lab that includes 3D printers, laser & vinyl cutting machines, as well as the ConneXion Satellite Library. Students are also welcome to study abroad and work at internships while studying as an undergraduate.

Notable Alumni

Denise Fleming and Marc Hansen

MINNEAPOLIS COLLEGE OF ART & DESIGN

Address: 2501 Stevens Avenue, Minneapolis, MN 55404
Website: *https://www.mcad.edu/academics/undergraduate/majors/illustration*
Contact: *https://mcad.edu/contact*
Phone: (612) 874-3700
Email: info@mcad.edu

COST OF ATTENDANCE:

Tuition & Fees: $49,452 | **Additional Expenses:** $7,640
Total: $57,092

Financial Aid: https://mcad.edu/admissions-and-aid/undergraduate/financial-aid

ADDITIONAL INFORMATION:

Available Degree(s)

- BFA Illustration
- Degrees BFA Comic Art

Portfolio Requirement

Portfolios are required for incoming students. Submit 8-16 works in any medium. Include the following four subjects: Landscape, Still Life, Interior Space, and Self-Portrait. At least one of these must be a drawing from direct observation. Include a full scale value. Submit via SlideRoom

Scholarships Offered

MCAD Admissions Merit Scholarships are available to all incoming students. In addition, the MCAD Annual Merit Scholarship is a competition for students currently enrolled full-time and who have a 3.0+ GPA. Furthermore, students may earn scholarships through national competitions such as ARTS and the Scholastic Art Awards that MCAD will match. These matching scholarships are need-based.

Special Opportunities

Illustration students explore traditional and alternative forms of illustration. Required coursework includes professional practice, digital illustration, tools of the trade, and more. At MCAD, illustration students are trained to create meaningful visual stories.

Notable Alumni

Adolf Dehn, Wanda Gág, Samara Golden, Mary GrandPré, M.S. Harkness, Dan Jurgens, Linus Maurer, Chris Monroe, Clara Elsene Peck, Eddie Perrote, Tania del Rio, and Pete Wagner

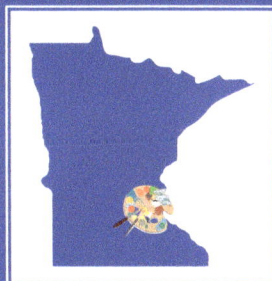

ILLINOIS

INDIANA

IOWA

KANSAS

MICHIGAN

MINNESOTA

MISSOURI

NEBRASKA

NORTH DAKOTA

OHIO

SOUTH DAKOTA

WISCONSIN

MIDWEST

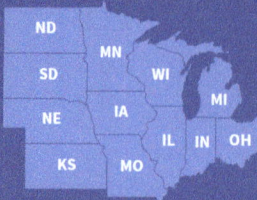

KANSAS CITY ART INSTITUTE

Address: 4415 Warwick Blvd., Kansas City, MO 64111
Website: *https://kcai.edu/academics/majors/illustration/*
Contact: *https://kcai.edu/contact-us/*
Phone: (800) 522-5224
Email: admiss@kcai.edu

COST OF ATTENDANCE:

Tuition & Fees: $41,174 | **Additional Expenses:** $17,210
Total: $58,384

Financial Aid: https://kcai.edu/financial-aid-scholarships/

ADDITIONAL INFORMATION:

Available Degree(s)

- BFA Illustration

Portfolio Requirement

Portfolios are required for incoming students. Submit at least 10 recent works. Submit via the student portal.

Scholarships Offered

KCAI merit scholarships are awarded to students annually as long as they maintain a cumulative GPA of 2.5+. In addition, the state of Missouri offers financial assistance grants to MO residents, such as Access Missouri and Bright Flight.

Special opportunities

At KCAI, students work with traditional and nontraditional methods to develop technical skills for the field. Students are required to work at an internship to gain professional experience. Illustration students take coursework in analytical drawing systems, story-telling, color and space, and more. KCAI also offers double majors in Art History/Illustration and Creative Writing/Illustration.

Notable Alumni

Paul Briggs, Richard Corbin, Marc Davis, Walt Disney, Jay Jackson, Barry Kooser, Jim Mahfood, Archer Prewitt, and Glen Rounds

ILLINOIS

INDIANA

IOWA

KANSAS

MICHIGAN

MINNESOTA

MISSOURI

NEBRASKA

NORTH DAKOTA

OHIO

SOUTH DAKOTA

WISCONSIN

WASHINGTON UNIVERSITY IN ST. LOUIS

Address: 1 Brookings Dr., St. Louis, MO 63130
Website: *https://samfoxschool.wustl.edu/academics/college-of-art/bfa-ba-in-studio-art-and-design/communication-design*
Contact: *https://admissions.wustl.edu/contact-us/*
Phone: (314) 935-5858
Email: admissions@wustl.edu

COST OF ATTENDANCE:

Tuition & Fees: $57,750 | **Additional Expenses:** $19,016
Total: $76,766

Financial Aid: https://financialaid.wustl.edu/

ADDITIONAL INFORMATION:

Available Degree(s)

- BFA Communication Design, emphasis: Illustration

Portfolio Requirement

Portfolios are required for incoming students. Submit 10-20 works via SlideRoom.

Scholarships Offered

WashU offers merit-based and need-based scholarships for students in any major. Some of these institutional scholarships cover the full cost of tuition. They also offer the Signature Scholar Program, which involves individual applications and a weekend program. Partial and full tuition are offered within this scholarship program.

Special Opportunities

There are no formal concentrations in the Communication Design major. However, students may informally emphasize their coursework in Illustration classes. Students learn advanced drawing techniques, visual storytelling, sketchbook practice, and how to develop their signature style. With no formal concentrations, students move between drawing, typography, graphic design, book arts, interaction design, and more.

Notable Alumni

Larry Cuba, Bernard Fuchs, Al Parker, Mike Peters, Dan Pirari, and Lauren Weinstein

ILLINOIS

INDIANA

IOWA

KANSAS

MICHIGAN

MINNESOTA

MISSOURI

NEBRASKA

NORTH DAKOTA

OHIO

SOUTH DAKOTA

WISCONSIN

MIDWEST

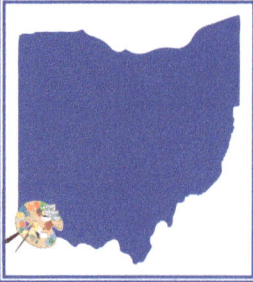

ILLINOIS

INDIANA

IOWA

KANSAS

MICHIGAN

MINNESOTA

MISSOURI

NEBRASKA

NORTH DAKOTA

OHIO

SOUTH DAKOTA

WISCONSIN

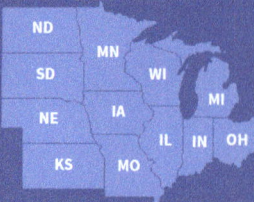

ART ACADEMY OF CINCINNATI

Address: 1212 Jackson St, Cincinnati, OH 45202
Website: *https://www.artacademy.edu/majors/illustration/illustration.php*
Contact: *https://www.artacademy.edu/contact.php*
Phone: (513) 562-6262
Email: admissions@artacademy.edu

COST OF ATTENDANCE:

Tuition & Fees: $35,500 | **Additional Expenses:** $6,100
Total: $41,600

Financial Aid: https://www.artacademy.edu/financial-aid/overview.php

ADDITIONAL INFORMATION:

Available Degree(s)

- BFA Illustration

Portfolio Requirement

Portfolios are required for incoming students. Submit 8-10 works via SlideRoom.

Scholarships Offered

Applicants accepted to any BFA program are eligible for the Entrance Scholarship. This scholarship is merit-based and requires a separate application. The total award is approximately $32,000 over four years. AAC also offers other first-year scholarships and external scholarships are available.

Special Opportunities

The Illustration program at Art Academy of Cincinnati is trans-disciplinary. Illustration students explore other media, such as animation, drawing, photography, painting, sound art, motion graphics, and installation. They learn about visual communication and narrative storytelling.

Notable Alumni

Derek Alderfer, Will Hillenbrand, Chrissy Hoppes, Chelsey Hughes, Bob Million, Eric Overman, Chris Sickels, Joe Slucher, and Andrew Tremblay

CLEVELAND INSTITUTE OF ART

Address: 11610 Euclid Avenue, Cleveland, OH 44106
Website: *https://www.cia.edu/academics/illustration*
Contact: *https://www.cia.edu/contact*
Phone: (216) 421-7000
Email: admissions@cia.edu

COST OF ATTENDANCE:

Tuition & Fees: $45,495 | **Additional Expenses:** $17,010
Total: $62,505

Financial Aid: https://www.cia.edu/admissions/financing-your-education

ADDITIONAL INFORMATION:

Available Degree(s)

- BFA Illustration

Portfolio Requirement

Portfolios are required for incoming students. Submit 12-20 works via SlideRoom. Sketchbook pages are highly encouraged. Do not include works copied from photographs.

Scholarships Offered

CIA offers renewable merit scholarships to undergraduate students. Students are automatically considered upon acceptance. Students who do not receive a merit scholarship may still be considered for a need-based CIA grant if they submit a FAFSA.

Special Opportunities

CIA's Engage Practice is a feature of the school that provides students with the opportunity to work on real-world projects with external clients while they complete their studies. Students gain professional experience that will help them tremendously post-graduation. Illustration students are given their own workspaces, which mimics the real-world setting of working at a firm.

Notable Alumni

Brian Azzarello, Brain Michael Bendis, Marc Brown, Amy Gardiner, Dennis Janke, Mary Ann Scherr, and Matthew Sweeney

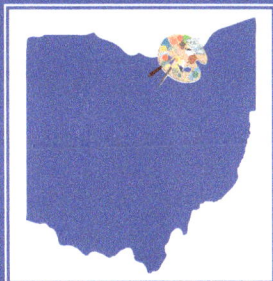

ILLINOIS

INDIANA

IOWA

KANSAS

MICHIGAN

MINNESOTA

MISSOURI

NEBRASKA

NORTH DAKOTA

OHIO

SOUTH DAKOTA

WISCONSIN

MIDWEST

ILLINOIS

INDIANA

IOWA

KANSAS

MICHIGAN

MINNESOTA

MISSOURI

NEBRASKA

NORTH DAKOTA

OHIO

SOUTH DAKOTA

WISCONSIN

COLUMBUS COLLEGE OF ART AND DESIGN

Address: 60 Cleveland Ave, Columbus, OH 43215
Website: *https://www.ccad.edu/academics/illustration*
Contact: *https://www.ccad.edu/directory*
Phone: (614) 224-9101
Email: admissions@ccad.edu

COST OF ATTENDANCE:

Tuition & Fees: $37,370 | **Additional Expenses:** $17,208
Total: $54,578

Financial Aid: https://www.ccad.edu/admissions/financial-aid

ADDITIONAL INFORMATION:

Available Degree(s)

- BFA Illustration
- BFA Comics & Narrative Practice

Portfolio Requirement

Portfolios are required for incoming students. Submit 8-15 works.

Scholarships Offered

CCAD offers academic and merit scholarships. There are also external scholarship opportunities, such as the Ohio Governor's Youth Art Exhibition, the Lounge Lizard scholarship competition, MVP Scholarships ($500) and more.

Special Opportunities

Illustration students at CCAD have access to the 3D illustration lab, the 2D illustration lab, the FabLab, printmaking lab, and computer lab. Equipment includes sculpting, casting, molding equipment, drawing tables, Cintiq monitors, light tables, 3D printers, laser cutters, spray booths, and a CNC machine.

Notable Alumni

Alan Becker, Roy Doty, Edward Mason Eggleston, Keron Grant, Nathan Greno, Kerry G. Johnson, Robert McCall, Jerry McDaniel, Ron Miller, John Jude Palencar, and Dan Scanlon

MILWAUKEE INSTITUTE OF ART & DESIGN

Address: 273 E Erie St, Milwaukee, WI 53202
Website: *https://www.miad.edu/academic-programs/degree-programs/illustration*
Contact: *https://www.miad.edu/about-miad/welcome/contact-us*
Phone: (414) 847-3200
Email: admissions@miad.edu

COST OF ATTENDANCE:

Tuition & Fees: $41,240 | **Additional Expenses:** $9,330
Total: $50,570

Financial Aid: https://www.miad.edu/financial-aid/overview/not-just-numbers

ADDITIONAL INFORMATION:

Available Degree(s)

- BFA Illustration

Portfolio Requirement

Portfolios are required for incoming students. Submit 12-20 works. Applicants must include works from direct observation rather than from imagination or copied.

Scholarships Offered

MIAD offers merit-based and need-based scholarships to all students. There is no separate application required. Merit scholarships range from $12,000 per year up to full tuition.

Special Opportunities

Illustration students experiment with various media, including digital and 3D art. Students are encouraged to develop their personal style. MIAD hosts the Illustration Seminar, a series of workshops presented by professionals. Students develop their professional portfolios by graduation.

Notable Alumni

Autumn Brown, Ryan Carter, Madeline Dall, Max Estes, Erica Lyn Huppe, Jenny Kim, Uriah Fracassi, Briana MacWilliam, Keith Negley, Adam Osgood, Rob Schrab, Scott Taylor, Tiffany Vancil, and Kevin Werth

ILLINOIS

INDIANA

IOWA

KANSAS

MICHIGAN

MINNESOTA

MISSOURI

NEBRASKA

NORTH DAKOTA

OHIO

SOUTH DAKOTA

WISCONSIN

MIDWEST

CHAPTER 13

REGION THREE

SOUTH

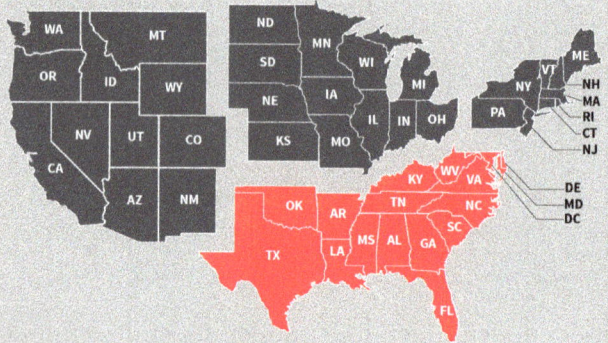

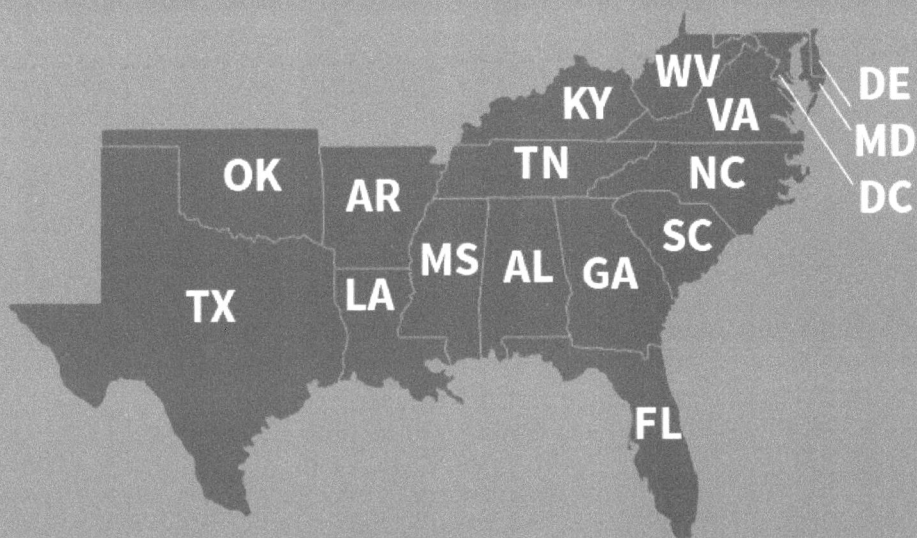

10 *Programs* | **16** *States*

1. *FL - Ringling College of Art and Design*
2. *FL – University of Central Florida*
3. *GA - Savannah College of Art and Design (SCAD)*
4. *GA - University of Georgia*
5. *MD - Maryland Institute College of Art*
6. *NC - East Carolina University*
7. *NC - University of North Carolina at Charlotte*
8. *TN - Belmont University*
9. *TX - Texas State University*
10. *VA - Virginia Commonwealth University*

ILLUSTRATION & COMIC ART PROGRAMS

School	Avg. GPA, SAT Evidence-Based Reading Writing (ERW), SAT Math (M), and ACT Composite (C) Early Decision (ED): Yes/No	Admission Statistics	Program(s)	Portfolio Required (req.)
Ringling College of Art & Design 2700 N. Tamiami Trail, Sarasota, FL 34234	GPA: N/A SAT (ERW): N/A* SAT (M): N/A* ACT (C): N/A* *Test-optional ED: No	Overall College Admit Rate: 69% Undergrad Enrollment: 1,624 Total Enrollment: 1,624	BFA Illustration	Portfolio req.
University of Central Florida 4000 Central Florida Blvd, Orlando, FL 32816	GPA: 4.16 SAT (ERW): 600-680 SAT (M): 570-670 ACT (C): 25-30 ED: No	Overall College Admit Rate: 36% Undergrad Enrollment: 60,075 Total Enrollment: 70,406	BFA Studio Art, specialization: Drawing and Illustration combination	Portfolio not req.
Savannah College of Art & Design (SCAD) 342 Bull St., Savannah, GA 31401	GPA: 3.6 SAT (ERW): 540-640 SAT (M): 500-600 ACT (C): 20-27 ED: No	Admit Rate: 78% Undergrad Enrollment: 11,679 Total Enrollment: 14,265	BFA Illustration	Portfolio req.
University of Georgia Dawson Hall, 305 Sanford Dr., Athens, GA 30602	GPA: 4.02 SAT (ERW): 620-700 SAT (M): 600-720 ACT (C): ED: No	Admit Rate: 48% Undergrad Enrollment: 29,765 Total Enrollment: 39,147	BFA Art, concentration: Scientific Illustration	Portfolio not req.

School	Avg. GPA, SAT Evidence-Based Reading Writing (ERW), SAT Math (M), and ACT Composite (C) Early Decision (ED): Yes/No	Admission Statistics	Program(s)	Portfolio Required (req.)
Maryland Institute College of Art (MICA) 1300 W. Mount Royal Ave., Baltimore, MD 21217	GPA: N/A SAT (ERW): N/A SAT (M): N/A ACT (C): N/A *Test-optional ED: Yes	Admit Rate: 90% Undergrad Enrollment: 1,331 Total Enrollment: 1,892	BFA Illustration	Portfolio req.
East Carolina University East 5th Street, Greenville, NC 27858	GPA: 3.28 SAT (ERW): 510-590 SAT (M): 510-580 ACT (C): 19-24 ED: No	Overall College Admit Rate: 88% Undergrad Enrollment: 23,056 Total Enrollment: 28,798	BFA Art, concentration: Illustration	Portfolio not req.
University of North Carolina at Charlotte 9201 University City Boulevard, Charlotte, NC 28223	GPA: 3.92 SAT (ERW): 560-640 SAT (M): 560-640 ACT (C): 22-27 ED: No	Overall College Admit Rate: 80% Undergrad Enrollment: 24,175 Total Enrollment: 30,146	BFA Art, concentration: Illustration	Portfolio req.
Belmont University 1900 Belmont Blvd, Nashville, TN 37212	GPA: 3.83 SAT (ERW): 580-660 SAT (M): 540-640 ACT (C): 23-30 ED: No	Overall College Admit Rate: 83% Undergrad Enrollment: 6,631 Total Enrollment: 8,204	BFA Illustration	Portfolio not req.

SOUTH

ILLUSTRATION & COMIC ART PROGRAMS

School	Avg. GPA, SAT Evidence-Based Reading Writing (ERW), SAT Math (M), and ACT Composite (C) Early Decision (ED): Yes/No	Admission Statistics	Program(s)	Portfolio Required (req.)
Texas State University 601 University Dr, San Marcos, TX 78666	GPA: N/A SAT (ERW): 510-600 SAT (M): 500-580 ACT (C): 20-25 ED: No	Overall College Admit Rate: 85% Undergrad Enrollment: 33,193 Total Enrollment: 37,812	BFA Communication Design, area of study: Illustration	Portfolio not req.
Virginia Commonwealth University Virginia Commonwealth University, Richmond, VA 23284	GPA: 3.72 SAT (ERW): 540-640 SAT (M): 520-610 ACT (C): 21-28 ED: No	Admit Rate: 91% Undergrad Enrollment: 21,943 Total Enrollment: 29,070	BFA Communication Arts, concentration: Scientific Illustration	Portfolio req.

ALABAMA

ARKANSAS

DELAWARE

DISTRICT OF
COLUMBIA

FLORIDA

GEORGIA

KENTUCKY

LOUISIANA

MARYLAND

MISSISSIPPI

NORTH CAROLINA

OKLAHOMA

SOUTH CAROLINA

TENNESSEE

TEXAS

VIRGINIA

WEST VIRGINIA

RINGLING COLLEGE OF ART & DESIGN

Address: 2700 N. Tamiami Trail, Sarasota, FL 34234
Website: *https://www.ringling.edu/illustration/*
Contact: *https://www.ringling.edu/contact*
Phone: (941) 351–5100
Email: admissions@ringling.edu

COST OF ATTENDANCE:

Tuition & Fees: $49,649 | **Additional Expenses:** $22,025
Total: $71,674

Financial Aid: https://www.ringling.edu/financialaid

ADDITIONAL INFORMATION:

Available Degree(s)

- BFA Illustration

Portfolio Requirement

Portfolios are required for incoming students. Submit via SlideRoom. Applicants must include drawings from observation. Copying other artists is not permitted. Applicants must also avoid cliches, such as anime, tattoos, dragons, or unicorns.

Scholarships Offered

Ringling College offers merit scholarships and need-based grants. Some of the scholarships include the Presidential Scholarship ($25,000 per year for 4 years), the Dean's Scholarship ($10,000 per year for 4 years), the Faculty Scholarship ($8,000 per year for 4 years) and several others.

Special Opportunities

Illustration students may choose to emphasize in General Illustration or Visual Development. In General Illustration, the goal is to create works that effectively communicate a message. In Visual Development, students are taught concept art, which is used by illustrators to convey ideas across the entertainment industry. Students learn to visualize and create character art that will later be used by modelers, visual effects artists, and other creatives.

Notable Alumni

John Marshall, Brandon Oldenburg, Patrick Osborne, and Mike Zeck

UNIVERSITY OF CENTRAL FLORIDA

Address: 4000 Central Florida Blvd, Orlando, FL 32816
Website: *https://svad.cah.ucf.edu/academics/studio-art/*
Contact: *https://www.ucf.edu/admissions/undergraduate/contact*
Phone: (844) 376-9160
Email: admission@ucf.edu

COST OF ATTENDANCE:

In-State Tuition & Fees: $5,944 | **Additional Expenses:** $16,180
Total: $22,124

Out-of-State Tuition & Fees: $20,969 | **Additional Expenses:** $16,180
Total: $37,149

Financial Aid: https://www.ucf.edu/services/s/financial-aid/

ADDITIONAL INFORMATION:

Available Degree(s)

- BFA Studio Art, specialization: Drawing and Illustration combination

Portfolio Requirement

Portfolios are not required for incoming students. Students submit a portfolio during their undergraduate years.

Scholarships Offered

All students are automatically considered for the Pegasus Scholarships. These merit-based scholarships are renewable and include the National Merit Scholarships, the Provost Scholarship, the Pegasus Gold, Silver, & Bronze Scholarships, and many more.

Special Opportunities

The BFA Studio Art major offers specializations in book arts, ceramics, drawing and printmaking combined, drawing and illustration combined, photography, sculpture, and type & design. University of Central Florida also offers a BA, which would allow the student to choose more than one specialization. The BFA is more studio-intensive.

Notable Alumni

Sara Lessans, Ren Sawyer, and Robert Venditti

ALABAMA
ARKANSAS
DELAWARE
DISTRICT OF COLUMBIA
FLORIDA
GEORGIA
KENTUCKY
LOUISIANA
MARYLAND
MISSISSIPPI
NORTH CAROLINA
OKLAHOMA
SOUTH CAROLINA
TENNESSEE
TEXAS
VIRGINIA
WEST VIRGINIA

SOUTH

SAVANNAH COLLEGE OF ART & DESIGN (SCAD)

ALABAMA

ARKANSAS

DELAWARE

DISTRICT OF COLUMBIA

FLORIDA

GEORGIA

KENTUCKY

LOUISIANA

MARYLAND

MISSISSIPPI

NORTH CAROLINA

OKLAHOMA

SOUTH CAROLINA

TENNESSEE

TEXAS

VIRGINIA

WEST VIRGINIA

Address: 342 Bull St., Savannah, GA 31401
Website: *https://www.scad.edu/academics/programs/illustration*
Contact: *https://www.scad.edu/about/contact*
Phone: (912) 525-5100
Email: contact@scad.edu
Other locations: Atlanta, GA

COST OF ATTENDANCE:

Tuition & Fees: $38,340 | **Additional Expenses:** $15,269
Total: $53,609

Financial Aid: https://www.scad.edu/admission/financial-aid-and-scholarships

ADDITIONAL INFORMATION:

Available Degree(s)

- BFA Illustration
- BFA Sequential Art

Portfolio Requirement

Portfolios are required for incoming students. Applicants may choose any of the following categories, whether or not it reflects their intended major: Business & Marketing, Visual Art, Time-Based Media, Writing, Equestrian, or Performing Arts. However, SCAD suggests applicants should curate a portfolio that demonstrates the applicant's interests and aptitude. Submit via SlideRoom.

Scholarships Offered

All applicants including international students are eligible for merit-scholarships. The May and Paul Poetter Scholarship awards full tuition and is based on academic achievement. The Frances Larkin McCommon Scholarship awards full tuition and is based on artistic achievement. SCAD also offers SCAD academic scholarships ($1,500-$12,000). Among grants, the SCAD Athletic Grant awards $2,000-$12,000. Furthermore, students may receive a scholarship award via the SCAD Challenge Scholarship. Awards range from $2,000-$4,000.

Special Opportunities

SCAD offers numerous minors that may be of interest to illustration majors, such as Animated Illustration and Publication Design, Scientific Illustration, Storyboarding, Illustration for Entertainment, and Illustration for Surface Design. Students may also earn a certificate in Digital Publishing. Related majors include Sequential Art and Graphic Design.

Notable Alumni

Robert Atkins, Luna Brothers, Jacen Burrows, Matt Davies, Eleanor Davis, Kristan Donaldson, Tom Feister, M. Alice LeGrow, Kelli Lee, Christy Lijewski, Sean Murphy, Malina Omut, Durwin Talon, Dean Trippe, Brett Weldele, Jarrett Williams, Jefferson Wood, and Tracy Yardley

UNIVERSITY OF GEORGIA

Address: Lamar Dodd School of Art, 270 River Road, Athens, GA 30602
Website: *https://art.uga.edu/academics/scientific-illustration*
Contact: *https://reg.uga.edu/general-information/contact-us/*
Phone: (706) 542-1511
Email: undergrad@admissions.uga.edu

COST OF ATTENDANCE:

In-State Tuition & Fees: $12,068 | **Additional Expenses:** $15,878
Total: $27,946

Out-of-State Tuition & Fees: $31,108 | **Additional Expenses:** $16,252
Total: $47,360

Financial Aid: https://osfa.uga.edu/

ADDITIONAL INFORMATION:

Available Degree(s)

- BFA Art, concentration: Scientific Illustration

Portfolio Requirement

Portfolios are not required for incoming students. However, students must undergo a portfolio review while they are undergraduate during the Fall or Spring semesters.

Scholarships Offered

The University of Georgia offers numerous academic-based, need-based, and both academic and need-based aids to students, many of which are open to Georgia residents, out-of-state students, and international students. Awards go as high as $22,900.

Special Opportunities

Accuracy and clear communication is significant in the field of scientific illustration. Students at University of Georgia learn just that. Students are educated on how to create diagrammatic illustrations that relate the message to the science student without confusing the viewer. Students in this concentration have access to drawing tables, a digital laboratory, stereomicroscopes, and more.

Notable Alumni

Jack Davis

ALABAMA
ARKANSAS
DELAWARE
DISTRICT OF COLUMBIA
FLORIDA
GEORGIA
KENTUCKY
LOUISIANA
MARYLAND
MISSISSIPPI
NORTH CAROLINA
OKLAHOMA
SOUTH CAROLINA
TENNESSEE
TEXAS
VIRGINIA
WEST VIRGINIA

SOUTH

MARYLAND INSTITUTE COLLEGE OF ART (MICA)

ALABAMA

ARKANSAS

DELAWARE

DISTRICT OF COLUMBIA

FLORIDA

GEORGIA

KENTUCKY

LOUISIANA

MARYLAND

MISSISSIPPI

NORTH CAROLINA

OKLAHOMA

SOUTH CAROLINA

TENNESSEE

TEXAS

VIRGINIA

WEST VIRGINIA

Address: 1300 W. Mount Royal Ave., Baltimore, MD 21217
Website: *https://www.mica.edu/undergraduate-majors-minors/illustration-major/*
Contact: *https://www.mica.edu/mica-dna/contact-us/*
Phone: (410) 669-9200
Email: https://www.mica.edu/forms/contact-undergraduate-admission/

COST OF ATTENDANCE:

Tuition & Fees: $53,333 | **Additional Expenses:** $17,820
Total: $71,153

Financial Aid: https://www.mica.edu/financial-aid/

ADDITIONAL INFORMATION:

Available Degree(s)

- BFA Illustration

Portfolio Requirement

Portfolios are required for incoming students. Submit 12-20 works. MICA strongly suggests including drawings from observation rather than from imagination or copied from photographs.

Scholarships Offered

MICA offers several, competitive merit-based scholarships to all incoming undergraduate students. Some of these offers include the Mathias J. Devito Scholarship Program ($40,000 over 4 years), the Fanny B. Thalheimer Scholarship ($16,000-$68,000 over four years), the Academic Excellence Scholarships ($12,000-$24,000) and several others.

Special Opportunities

Illustration students may choose a concentration in Illustration Studio, Book Arts, or Sequential Art. Students are taught digital and traditional approaches to the field. They are also taught problem-solving skills and entrepreneurial skills for professional work outside of the classroom.

Notable Alumni

Jeremy Caniglia, Jennifer Daniel, Shelby Shackelford, ND Stevenson, Babs Tarr, Annie Wu, and Lee Woodward Zeigler

EAST CAROLINA UNIVERSITY

Address: East 5th Street, Greenville, NC 27858
Website: *https://art.ecu.edu/undergraduate/*
Contact: *https://admissions.ecu.edu/connect/*
Phone: (252) 328-6640
Email: admissions@ecu.edu

COST OF ATTENDANCE:

In-State Tuition & Fees: $7,325 | **Additional Expenses:** $16,488
Total: $23,813

Out-of-State Tuition & Fees: $23,602 | **Additional Expenses:** $16,488
Total: $40,090

Financial Aid: https://financialaid.ecu.edu/

ADDITIONAL INFORMATION:

Available Degree(s)

- BFA Art, concentration: Illustration

Portfolio Requirement

Portfolios are not required for incoming students. However, they are during the second year, when students must undergo a portfolio review to apply for their concentration of choice.

Scholarships Offered

Students may apply for scholarships via the scholarship portal, ECUAward each year in August. There are a variety of external merit-based and need-based scholarships.

Special Opportunities

BFA Art students choose their area of concentration in their second year. Students are still encouraged to explore other areas of art within the degree, and coursework is also available in book arts, letterpress, glass, wood design, and interdisciplinary studios.

Notable Alumni

Jordan Thomas Cunningham, Joey Ellis, Mike Litwi, Nikolas McKeever, Madalyn McLeod, Bethany Salisbury, Eric Terry, and Trevor Van Meter

ALABAMA

ARKANSAS

DELAWARE

DISTRICT OF
COLUMBIA

FLORIDA

GEORGIA

KENTUCKY

LOUISIANA

MARYLAND

MISSISSIPPI

NORTH CAROLINA

OKLAHOMA

SOUTH CAROLINA

TENNESSEE

TEXAS

VIRGINIA

WEST VIRGINIA

SOUTH

UNIVERSITY OF NORTH CAROLINA AT CHARLOTTE

Address: 9201 University City Boulevard, Charlotte, NC 28223
Website: *https://catalog.charlotte.edu/preview_program. php?catoid=29&poid=8264*
Contact: *https://admissions.charlotte.edu/admissions-counselors*
Phone: (704) 687-5507
Email: admissions@uncc.edu

COST OF ATTENDANCE:

In-State Tuition & Fees: $7,188 | **Additional Expenses:** $16,528
Total: $23,716

Out-of-State Tuition & Fees: $20,622 | **Additional Expenses:** $17,436
Total: $38,058

Financial Aid: https://www.uncc.edu/landing/admissions-financial-aid

ADDITIONAL INFORMATION:

Available Degree(s)

- BFA Art, concentration: Illustration

Portfolio Requirement

Portfolios are required for incoming students. Submit 10 works.

Scholarships Offered

Students must apply for scholarships separately through the NinerScholars Portal. They are matched with scholarships and given directions on how to apply to individual awards. UNC Charlotte also encourages applying to external scholarships.

Special Opportunities

The Department of Art & Art History strongly recommends students study abroad. The recurring Rome summer program is a popular choice for students. Students may take up to five courses, including Photographing the Streets of Rome, Italian Language, Filmmaking, Mapping Rome, and Rome: City as History, City as Memory.

Notable Alumni

Melissa Agostini and Adam Bastuscheck

ALABAMA

ARKANSAS

DELAWARE

DISTRICT OF COLUMBIA

FLORIDA

GEORGIA

KENTUCKY

LOUISIANA

MARYLAND

MISSISSIPPI

NORTH CAROLINA

OKLAHOMA

SOUTH CAROLINA

TENNESSEE

TEXAS

VIRGINIA

WEST VIRGINIA

BELMONT UNIVERSITY

Address: 1900 Belmont Blvd, Nashville, TN 37212
Website: *https://www.belmont.edu/watkins/undergrad/illustration/index.html*
Contact: *https://www.belmont.edu/admissions/index.html*
Phone: (615) 460-6000
Email: N/A

COST OF ATTENDANCE:

Tuition & Fees: $38,430 | **Additional Expenses:** $19,875
Total: $58,305

Financial Aid: https://www.belmont.edu/sfs/aid/undergrad.html

ADDITIONAL INFORMATION:

Available Degree(s)

- BFA Illustration

Portfolio Requirement

Portfolios are not required for incoming students. They are required for certain merit-based scholarships. Submit 20 works.

Scholarships Offered

All applicants are automatically considered for merit scholarships when they submit their Belmont University application. Students who apply as test-optional will be considered for merit scholarships based on their high school GPA and overall strength of their application. General Freshman Academic Merit Scholarships ($3,000 to $10,000 annually) are awarded on a rolling basis following the offer of admission. Belmont also offers named awards, which recognize approximately the top two percent of all freshman applicants.

Special Opportunities

Illustration students at Belmont focus on developing their technical skills, visual storytelling abilities, and curating a keen entrepreneurial focus. Students take coursework in visual literacy, graphic design, typography, professional development, and service learning. Students also may learn editorial design, character design, art licensing, advertising illustration, and more.

Notable Alumni

Mary Spaar

ALABAMA

ARKANSAS

DELAWARE

DISTRICT OF COLUMBIA

FLORIDA

GEORGIA

KENTUCKY

LOUISIANA

MARYLAND

MISSISSIPPI

NORTH CAROLINA

OKLAHOMA

SOUTH CAROLINA

TENNESSEE

TEXAS

VIRGINIA

WEST VIRGINIA

SOUTH

TEXAS STATE UNIVERSITY

Address: 601 University Dr, San Marcos, TX 78666
Website: *https://www.finearts.txstate.edu/Art/academics/ undergrad/ugrad-comdes.html*
Contact: *https://www.theatreanddance.txstate.edu/About-the-Department/Contact-Us.html*
Phone: (512) 245-2111
Email: https://www.admissions.txstate.edu/contact.html

COST OF ATTENDANCE:

In-State Tuition & Fees: $11,540 | **Additional Expenses:** $15,080
Total: $26,620

Out-of-State Tuition & Fees: $23,820 | **Additional Expenses:** $15,080
Total: $38,900

Financial Aid: https://www.finaid.txstate.edu/

ADDITIONAL INFORMATION:

Available Degree(s)

- BFA Communication Design, area of study: Illustration

Portfolio Requirement

Portfolios are not required for incoming students. However, students must pass three art courses at Texas State and undergo a portfolio year after their first year in order to be fully admitted to the program.

Scholarships Offered

Out-of-state students may qualify for a nonresident tuition waiver if they, "qualify for at least $1,000 in Texas State competitive or merit scholarships…". In addition, all applicants are automatically awarded National Scholarships and Assured scholarships when they gain acceptance to TSU. A number of competitive scholarships are available as well.

Special Opportunities

Texas State's Communication Design program has strong ties with national organizations that allow their students to gain internships, mentoring, and shadowing opportunities. Students have opportunities for networking and improve their professional skills while also building their technical skills in illustration.

Notable Alumni

Taylor Cole, Markel Lee, and Morgan Thomas

VIRGINIA COMMONWEALTH UNIVERSITY

Address: Virginia Commonwealth University, Richmond, VA 23284
Website: *https://arts.vcu.edu/academics/departments/communication-arts/*
Contact: *https://www.vcu.edu/contacts/*
Phone: (804) 828-0100
Email: ugrad@vcu.edu

COST OF ATTENDANCE:

In-State Tuition & Fees: $17,140 | **Additional Expenses:** $17,549
Total: $34,689

Out-of-State Tuition & Fees: $38,478 | **Additional Expenses:** $17,549
Total: $56,027

Financial Aid: https://finaid.vcu.edu/

ADDITIONAL INFORMATION:

Available Degree(s)

- BFA Communication Arts

Portfolio Requirement

Portfolios are required for incoming students. Submit 12-16 works created over the past two years. Applicants are encouraged to include drawings from observation and discouraged to include copied work.

Scholarships Offered

First-year students may be eligible for VCUarts talent scholarships ($5,000-$12,000 annually) if they apply by January 15th. Students are automatically considered and eligibility is based on academic merit and artistic talent. In addition, all students are automatically considered for institutional scholarships if they apply by November 15th. University scholarship awards vary based on the scholarship, but range from $8,000 per year to $16,000 plus room and board per year.

Special Opportunities

The Communication Arts major prepares students for work as a character designer, illustrator for print or digital publishing, a comic book artist, or a scientific illustrator. VCU offers an official concentration in Scientific Illustration. Coursework includes Imagery for Children, 3D Modeling for Concept Design, Game Design, Theory and Practice, Imagery for Science Fiction and Fantasy, and more.

Notable Alumni

Sterling Hundley, Wiley Miller, Steve Segal, Alice Tangerini, Phil Trumbo, Charles Vess, and Mike Wieringo

ALABAMA

ARKANSAS

DELAWARE

DISTRICT OF COLUMBIA

FLORIDA

GEORGIA

KENTUCKY

LOUISIANA

MARYLAND

MISSISSIPPI

NORTH CAROLINA

OKLAHOMA

SOUTH CAROLINA

TENNESSEE

TEXAS

VIRGINIA

WEST VIRGINIA

SOUTH

CHAPTER 14

REGION FOUR

WEST

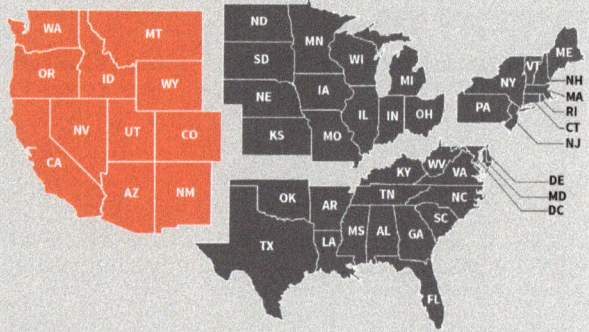

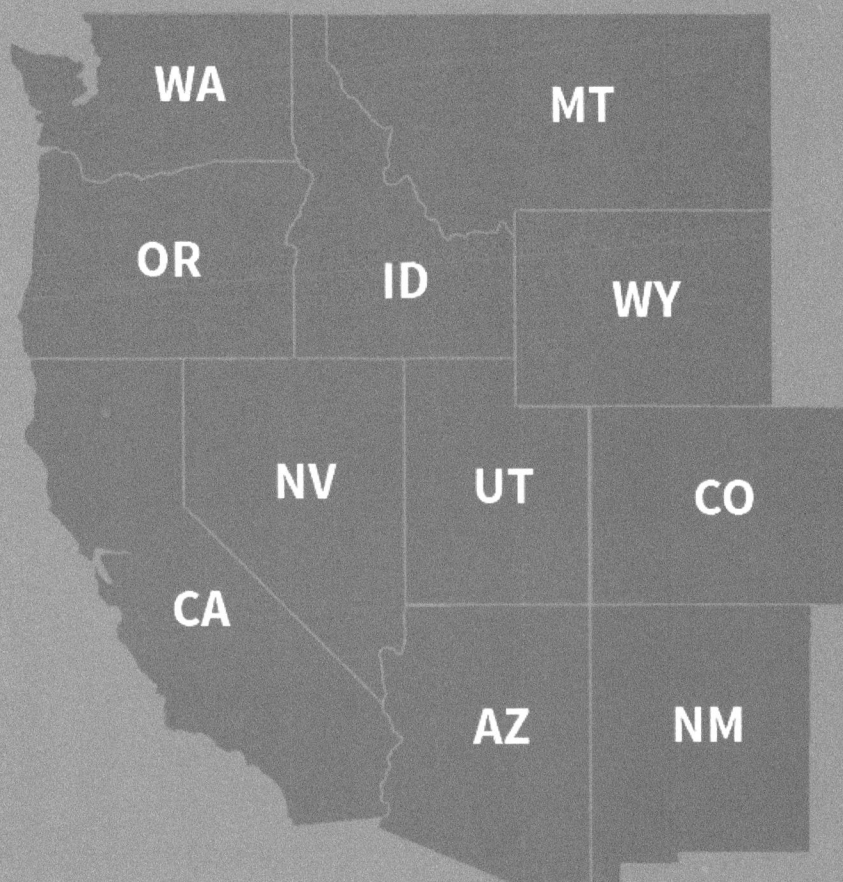

14 *Programs* | **13** *States*

1. *AZ - University of Arizona*
2. *CA - Academy of Art University*
3. *CA - ArtCenter College of Design*
4. *CA - California College of the Arts (CCA)*
5. *CA - California State University, Fullerton*
6. *CA - California State University, Long Beach*
7. *CA - California State University, Northridge*
8. *CA - Laguna College of Art and Design*
9. *CA - Otis College of Art and Design*
10. *CA - San José State University (SJSU)*
11. *CO - Rocky Mountain College of Art and Design*
12. *CO - University of Colorado, Denver*
13. *OR - Pacific Northwest College of Art*
14. *UT - Brigham Young University*

School	Avg. GPA, SAT Evidence-Based Reading Writing (ERW), SAT Math (M), and ACT Composite (C) Early Decision (ED): Yes/No	Admission Statistics	Program(s)	Portfolio Required (req.)
University of Arizona 1040 N. Olive Rd., Tucson, AZ 85721	GPA: 3.43 SAT (ERW): 550-660 SAT (M): 540-690 ACT (C): 21-29 ED: No	Overall College Admit Rate: 85% Undergrad Enrollment: 36,503 Total Enrollment: 46,932	BFA Studio Art, emphasis: Illustration & Design	Portfolio req.
Academy of Art University 79 New Montgomery St., San Francisco, CA 94105	GPA: N/A SAT (ERW): N/A SAT (M): N/A ACT (C): N/A *Academy of Art has an open admissions policy. ED: No	Admit Rate: N/A Undergrad Enrollment: 6,124 Total Enrollment: 8,928	BFA Illustration	Portfolio not req.
ArtCenter College of Design 1700 Lida St, Pasadena, CA 91103	GPA: N/A SAT (ERW): N/A* SAT (M): N/A* ACT (C): N/A* *Test-optional ED: No	Overall College Admit Rate: 76% Undergrad Enrollment: 1,912 Total Enrollment: 2,182	BFA Illustration	Portfolio req.
California College of the Arts (CCA) 1111 Eighth St., San Francisco, CA 94107	GPA: N/A SAT (ERW): N/A* SAT (M): N/A* ACT (C): N/A* *Test-optional ED: No	Overall College Admit Rate: 85% Undergrad Enrollment: 1,239 Total Enrollment: 1,612	BFA Illustration	Portfolio req.

School	Avg. GPA, SAT Evidence-Based Reading Writing (ERW), SAT Math (M), and ACT Composite (C) Early Decision (ED): Yes/No	Admission Statistics	Program(s)	Portfolio Required (req.)
California State University, Fullerton (CSUF) 800 N State College Blvd, Fullerton, CA 92831	GPA: N/A SAT (ERW): 500-590 SAT (M): 500-590 ACT (C): 18-23 ED: No	Overall College Admit Rate: 68% Undergrad Enrollment: 36,975 Total Enrollment: 42,051	BFA Art, concentration: Illustration	Portfolio not req.
California State University, Long Beach (CSULB) 1250 Bellflower Boulevard, Long Beach, CA 90840	GPA: 3.68 SAT (ERW): 510-620 SAT (M): 510-620 ACT (C): 20-26 ED: No	Admit Rate: 42% Undergrad Enrollment: 34,216 Total Enrollment: 40,069	BFA Studio Art, track: Illustration	Portfolio not req.
California State University, Northridge (CSUN) 18111 Nordhoff Street, Northridge, CA 91330	GPA: 3.39 SAT (ERW): 460-560 SAT (M): 440-550 ACT (C): 16-22 ED: No	Admit Rate: 66% Undergrad Enrollment: 34,916 Total Enrollment: 40,381	BA Visual Arts, concentration: Illustration	Portfolio not req.
Laguna College of Art and Design 2222 Laguna Canyon Rd., Laguna Beach, CA 92651	GPA: N/A SAT (ERW): 710-760 SAT (M): 770-800 ACT (C): 34-36 ED: No	Admit Rate: 83% Undergrad Enrollment: 732 Total Enrollment: 782	BFA Illustration	Portfolio req.

WEST

ILLUSTRATION & COMIC ART PROGRAMS

School	Avg. GPA, SAT Evidence-Based Reading Writing (ERW), SAT Math (M), and ACT Composite (C) Early Decision (ED): Yes/No	Admission Statistics	Program(s)	Portfolio Required (req.)
Otis College of Art and Design 9045 Lincoln Blvd., Los Angeles, CA 90045	GPA: N/A SAT (ERW): N/A SAT (M): N/A ACT (C): N/A *Test-optional ED: No	Admit Rate: 80% Undergrad Enrollment: 1,030 Total Enrollment: 1,073	BFA Communication Arts, emphasis: Illustration	Portfolio req.
San José State University (SJSU) One Washington Square, San José, CA 95192	GPA: N/A SAT (ERW): 500-640 SAT (M): 520-680 ACT (C): 20-31 ED: No	Admit Rate: 84% Undergrad Enrollment: 28,201 Total Enrollment: 33,808	BFA Animation & Illustration	Portfolio not req.
Rocky Mountain College of Art and Design 1600 Pierce Street, Denver, CO, 80214	GPA: N/A SAT (ERW): N/A* SAT (M): N/A* ACT (C): N/A* *Test-optional ED: No	Admit Rate: N/A Undergrad Enrollment: 1,631 Total Enrollment: 1,643	BFA Illustration	Portfolio req.
University of Colorado, Denver 1201 Larimer St, Denver, CO 80204	GPA: N/A SAT (ERW): 490-610 SAT (M): 510-600 ACT (C): 22-27 ED: No	Admit Rate: 66% Undergrad Enrollment: 14,994 Total Enrollment: 24,723	BFA Visual Arts, emphasis: Illustration	Portfolio not req.

School	Avg. GPA, SAT Evidence-Based Reading Writing (ERW), SAT Math (M), and ACT Composite (C) Early Decision (ED): Yes/No	Admission Statistics	Program(s)	Portfolio Required (req.)
Pacific Northwest College of Art 511 NW Broadway, Portland, OR 97209	GPA: N/A SAT (ERW): N/A* SAT (M): N/A* ACT (C): N/A* *Test-optional ED: No	Admit Rate: 96% Undergrad Enrollment: 445 Total Enrollment: 569	BFA Illustration	Portfolio req.
Brigham Young University Brigham Young University, Provo, UT 84602	GPA: 3.86 SAT (ERW): 610-700 SAT (M): 590-710 ACT (C): 26-32 ED: No	Admit Rate: 69% Undergrad Enrollment: 33,365 Total Enrollment: 36,450	BFA Illustration	Portfolio req.

WEST

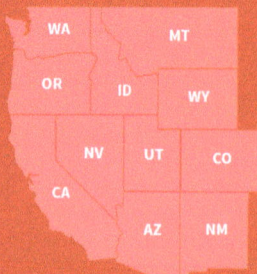

UNIVERSITY OF ARIZONA

Address: 1040 N. Olive Rd., Tucson, AZ 85721
Website: *https://art.arizona.edu/prospective-students/areas-of-study/illustration-design/*
Contact: *https://www.arizona.edu/contact-us*
Phone: (520) 621-6751
Email: admissions@arizona.edu

COST OF ATTENDANCE:

In-State Tuition & Fees: $12,700 | **Additional Expenses:** $18,050
Total: $30,750

Out-of-State Tuition & Fees: $37,200 | **Additional Expenses:** $18,050
Total: $55,250

Financial Aid: https://financialaid.arizona.edu/

ADDITIONAL INFORMATION:

Available Degree(s)

- BFA Studio Art, emphasis: Illustration & Design

Portfolio Requirement

Portfolios are required for incoming students. Submit 8 works. Students applying for the Illustration + Design program must also pass a secondary portfolio review after their first year.

Scholarships Offered

University of Arizona offers several merit-based and need-based awards. Arizona residents are eligible for the Resident Wildcat Awards, based on GPA and test scores. Awards range from $3,000-$15,000. The Non-Resident Arizona Awards range from $2,000-$35,000.

Special Opportunities

Faculty in the Illustration + Design program have expertise in letterpress, book arts, visual narratives, motion graphics, and more. The program is highly interdisciplinary, with students exploring various media to inform their personal style. Internships, field trips, team projects, study abroad, and community clients are all opportunities for students. Students are also required to have a portfolio and web presence to prepare them for work post-graduation.

Notable Alumni

Jeff Barfoot, Eric Boelts, Rich Borge, Jeff Lowry, Rob Nicoletti, Brian Stauffer, Kerry Stratford, and Margaret Youngblood

ACADEMY OF ART UNIVERSITY

Address: 79 New Montgomery St., San Francisco, CA 94105
Website: *https://www.academyart.edu/degree/illustration/?degree=bfa*
Contact: *https://my.academyart.edu/directories/admissions*
Phone: (800) 544-2787
Email: admissions@academyart.edu

COST OF ATTENDANCE:

Tuition & Fees: $26,399 | **Additional Expenses:** N/A
Total: $26,399

Financial Aid: https://www.academyart.edu/finances/types-of-financial-aid/

ADDITIONAL INFORMATION:

Available Degree(s)

- BFA Illustration

Portfolio Requirement

Portfolios are not required for incoming students.

Scholarships Offered

The Emerging Artist Scholarship offers awards up to $3,000. International Art & Design Scholarship awards a limited number of scholarships (up to $2,000) to international students.

Special Opportunities

Illustration students at Academy of Art take coursework such as Clothed Figure Drawing, Introduction to Anatomy, Digital Media, Writing the Short Story, Graphic Novel/Comic Book, Physics for Artists, and more. They build their technical skills and professional skills as they craft their portfolio.

Notable Alumni

Robert Hunt and David Markowitz

ALASKA

ARIZONA

CALIFORNIA

COLORADO

HAWAII

IDAHO

MONTANA

NEVADA

NEW MEXICO

OREGON

UTAH

WASHINGTON

WYOMING

WEST

ALASKA

ARIZONA

CALIFORNIA

COLORADO

HAWAII

IDAHO

MONTANA

NEVADA

NEW MEXICO

OREGON

UTAH

WASHINGTON

WYOMING

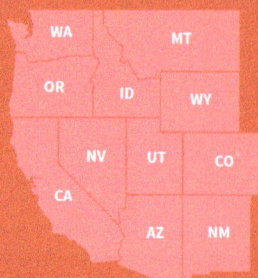

ARTCENTER COLLEGE OF DESIGN

Address: 1700 Lida St, Pasadena, CA 91103
Website: *https://www.artcenter.edu/academics/undergraduate-degrees/illustration/overview.html*
Contact: *http://www.artcenter.edu/admissions/contact.html*
Phone: (626) 396-2373
Email: admissions@artcenter.edu

COST OF ATTENDANCE:

Tuition & Fees: $49,653 | **Additional Expenses:** $24,820
Total: $74,473

Financial Aid: https://www.artcenter.edu/admissions/tuition-and-aid/tuition-and-fees/tuition.html

ADDITIONAL INFORMATION:

Available Degree(s)

- BFA Illustration

Portfolio Requirement

Portfolios are required for incoming students. Submit 20-25 drawings or paintings. Within your portfolio, 8-12 must be figure drawings from a live model, 8-10 must be imaginative pieces, and 5-6 should be pages from your sketchbook.

Scholarships Offered

ArtCenter awards merit-based and need-based scholarships to students. Students with an exceptional portfolio are awarded up to $25,000.

Special Opportunities

Illustration students start their training by mastering foundational skills in figure drawing, painting, and perspective. Then, they choose from one of five areas of specialization: Illustration Design, Illustration/Fine Art, Entertainment Arts, Entertainment Arts Consumer Products, Motion Design and Surface Design.

Notable Alumni

Peter Brown, Justin Bua, Marc Burckhardt, Ricardo Delgado, Marla Frazee, Grace Lynne Haynes, Philip Hays, Bob Jones, Rafael López, Richard MacDonald, Matt Mahurin, Mick McGinty, Andy Park, Tara McPherson, Floyd Norman, John Parra, LeUyen Pham, Robert Quackenbush, Walter Rane, Marc Remus, Dan Santat, Alex Schaefer, Lane Smith, Barron Storey, Drew Struzan, Ray Turner, and Michael Whelan

CALIFORNIA COLLEGE OF THE ARTS (CCA)

Address: 1111 Eighth St., San Francisco, CA 94107
Website: *https://www.cca.edu/design/illustration/*
Contact: *Contact via phone or email.*
Phone: (800) 447-1278
Email: info@cca.edu

COST OF ATTENDANCE:

Tuition & Fees: $54,726 | **Additional Expenses:** $25,255
Total: $79,981

Financial Aid: https://www.cca.edu/admissions/tuition/#section-financial-aid

ADDITIONAL INFORMATION:

Available Degree(s)

- BFA Illustration

Portfolio Requirement

Portfolios are required for incoming students. Submit 10-15 works via SlideRoom.

Scholarships Offered

Merit-based, need-based, CCA-named, and other scholarships available.

Special Opportunities

At CCA, students develop a strong foundation in drawing and painting. They learn how to use various mediums, such as charcoal, colored pencil, gouache, ink, acrylic, watercolor, and more. They learn technical skills in brush techniques, screenprinting, hand-lettering, sculpting, and color mixing.

Notable Alumni

Patrick Arrasmith, Tomie dePaola, Dave Gonzales, Mike Mignola, Lee Mingwei, Jey Parks, and Steve Purcell

ALASKA

ARIZONA

CALIFORNIA

COLORADO

HAWAII

IDAHO

MONTANA

NEVADA

NEW MEXICO

OREGON

UTAH

WASHINGTON

WYOMING

WEST

ALASKA

ARIZONA

CALIFORNIA

COLORADO

HAWAII

IDAHO

MONTANA

NEVADA

NEW MEXICO

OREGON

UTAH

WASHINGTON

WYOMING

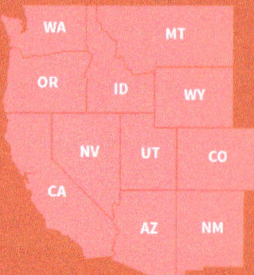

CALIFORNIA STATE UNIVERSITY, FULLERTON (CSUF)

Address: 800 N State College Blvd, Fullerton, CA 92831
Website: *https://www.fullerton.edu/arts/Art/students/va-roadmaps/bfa-illustration.php*
Contact: *http://admissions.fullerton.edu/contact.php*
Phone: (657) 278-3100
Email: admissions@fullerton.edu

COST OF ATTENDANCE:

In-State Tuition & Fees: $6,870 | **Additional Expenses:** $20,912
Total: $27,782

Out-of-State Tuition & Fees: $16,358 | **Additional Expenses:** $20,492
Total: $36,850

Financial Aid: https://www.fullerton.edu/financialaid/

ADDITIONAL INFORMATION:

Available Degree(s)

- BFA Art, concentration: Illustration

Portfolio Requirement

Portfolios are not required for incoming students. However, to proceed with the BFA degree, students must undergo a portfolio review during their time as an undergraduate.

Scholarships Offered

Merit-based and need-based scholarships are available at CSUF. Award amounts vary.

Special Opportunities

CSUF Illustration students take coursework in lettering & typography, perspective drawing, 3D computer animation, narrative illustration, sequential art, and more.

Notable Alumni

Farnaz Esnaashari-Charmatz, Dan Kitchens, Kozue Kitchens, Patrick Nagel, and Fred Tomaselli

CALIFORNIA STATE UNIVERSITY, LONG BEACH

Address: 1250 Bellflower Boulevard, Long Beach, CA 90840
Website: *https://www.csulb.edu/school-of-art/areas-of-study/studio-art/illustration-animation*
Contact: *https://www.csulb.edu/contact*
Phone: (562) 985-4111
Email: https://www.csulb.edu/contact

COST OF ATTENDANCE:

In-State Tuition & Fees: $6,846 | Additional Expenses: $18,206
Total: $25,386

Out-of-State Tuition & Fees: $17,142 | **Additional Expenses:** $18,540
Total: $35,682

Financial Aid: https://www.csulb.edu/student-affairs/financial-aid-and-scholarships-office

ADDITIONAL INFORMATION:

Available Degree(s)

- BFA Studio Art, track: Illustration

Portfolio Requirement

Portfolios are not required for incoming students. However, to proceed with the BFA degree, students must undergo a portfolio review during their time as an undergraduate.

Scholarships Offered

The President's Scholars Program offers merit-based scholarships to students admitted to the University Honors Program (UHP). Students may apply for BeachScholarships once they are admitted into CSULB.

Special Opportunities

Drawing from observation is a foundational skill necessary for Illustration students. Students who opt for the Illustration track take their courses along the Animation track students. All students have access to the digital lab and learn basic technical skills and professional skills as well.

Notable Alumni

Chris Bachalo, Roberta Gergory, and Scott Stantis

ALASKA

ARIZONA

CALIFORNIA

COLORADO

HAWAII

IDAHO

MONTANA

NEVADA

NEW MEXICO

OREGON

UTAH

WASHINGTON

WYOMING

WEST

ALASKA

ARIZONA

CALIFORNIA

COLORADO

HAWAII

IDAHO

MONTANA

NEVADA

NEW MEXICO

OREGON

UTAH

WASHINGTON

WYOMING

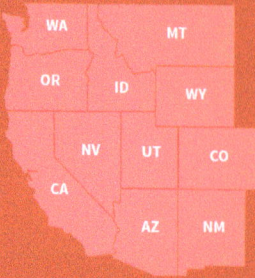

CALIFORNIA STATE UNIVERSITY, NORTHRIDGE (CSUN)

Address: 18111 Nordhoff Street, Northridge, CA 91330
Website: *https://www.csun.edu/mike-curb-arts-media-communication/art/illustration*
Contact: *https://www.csun.edu/contact*
Phone: (818) 677-1200
Email: outreach.recruitment.@csun.edu

COST OF ATTENDANCE:

In-State Tuition & Fees: $6,972 | **Additional Expenses:** $16,670
Total: $23,642

Out-of-State Tuition & Fees: $16,476 | **Additional Expenses:** $16,670
Total: $33,146

Financial Aid: https://www.csun.edu/financialaid/financial-aid-basics

ADDITIONAL INFORMATION:

Available Degree(s)

- BA Visual Arts, concentration: Illustration

Portfolio Requirements

Portfolios are not required for incoming students.

Scholarships Offered

CSUN offers several different scholarships to incoming students. It is suggested that students look through current scholarship opportunities, as they are constantly changing.

Special Opportunities

Illustration students at CSUN study art as a form and as a profession. Coursework covers historical and contemporary illustration practices, self-promotion and business skills, portfolio and website development, and more. CSUN also hosts a figure drawing workshop for university students and the general public.

Notable Alumni

Greg Evans and Andy Luckey

LAGUNA COLLEGE OF ART AND DESIGN

Address: 2222 Laguna Canyon Rd., Laguna Beach, CA 92651
Website: *https://www.lcad.edu/program/illustration*
Contact: *https://www.lcad.edu/contact*
Phone: (949) 376-6000
Email: admissions@lcad.edu

COST OF ATTENDANCE:

Tuition & Fees: $32,600 | **Additional Expenses:** $23,979
Total: $56,579

Financial Aid: https://www.lcad.edu/admissions/tuition-financial-aid/financial-aid

ADDITIONAL INFORMATION:

Available Degree(s)

- BFA Illustration

Portfolio Requirement

Portfolios are required for incoming students. Submit 12-20 recent works. LCAD suggests including observational works, life drawings, environmental works, renderings from a photographic reference, sequential illustrations, and creative problem solving work.

Scholarships Offered

The LCAD Institutional Grant is a merit-based scholarship that is based on academics and the admissions portfolio. This scholarship is renewable each year the student is at LCAD provided they remain in good academic standing. It is recommended that students apply for outside scholarships as well.

Special Opportunities

At LCAD, illustration students are taught how to master technical skills and present work for fields such as children's books, comics, gallery art, graphic novels, product design, science fields, fashion, industrial design, and more. Alumni have worked at Blizzard Entertainment, Google, Hurley, DreamWorks Animation, Disney Interactive, Warner Bros, MARVEL Entertainment, and more.

Notable Alumni

Katy Betz, Jessica Bulinski, Henry Cram, Ryan Darling, Lydia Fenwick, Scott Gordon, Kellie Hautala, Ashleigh Izienicki, Amy Kells, Monica Magala, Michael Savas, Beau Stanton, and Ben Thompson

ALASKA

ARIZONA

CALIFORNIA

COLORADO

HAWAII

IDAHO

MONTANA

NEVADA

NEW MEXICO

OREGON

UTAH

WASHINGTON

WYOMING

WEST

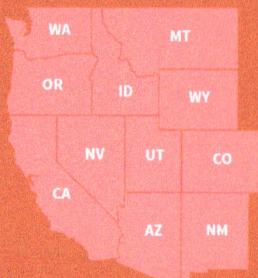

OTIS COLLEGE OF ART AND DESIGN

Address: 9045 Lincoln Blvd., Los Angeles, CA 90045
Website: *https://www.otis.edu/illustration*
Contact: *https://www.otis.edu/contact-otis-college-art-design*
Phone: (310) 665-6800
Email: admissions@otis.edu

COST OF ATTENDANCE:

Tuition & Fees: $47,700 | **Additional Expenses:** $21,354
Total: $69,054

Financial Aid: https://www.otis.edu/financial-aid

ADDITIONAL INFORMATION:

Available Degree(s)

- BFA Communication Arts, emphasis: Illustration

Portfolio Requirement

Portfolios are required for incoming students. Applicants may choose one of two options for their portfolio submission: Open or Structured. The open portfolio requires 10-20 recent works. The structured portfolio requires 3 images of portraits without showing the person's face, 4 images that tell a story, and 3 images that show places of importance to you.

Scholarships Offered

Otis College Scholarships are awarded to students based on need, academic merit, and artistic merit. Otis Named Scholarships are awarded by donors such as Nike or Sony for students who maintain a 3.0+ GPA and typically require a recommendation from the department chair. Otis College also recommends students apply for outside scholarships.

Special Opportunities

Illustration majors at Otis College develop a strong personal style during their undergraduate studies. Otis College prepares their students for work as professional illustrators, art directors, storyboard artists, comic book writers, children's book illustrators, muralists, and more. Advertising Design is a popular minor for these students.

Notable Alumni

Patrick Ching, Bob Clampett, Robert Day, Lawrence Lindell, and Joseph Mugnaini

ALASKA

ARIZONA

CALIFORNIA

COLORADO

HAWAII

IDAHO

MONTANA

NEVADA

NEW MEXICO

OREGON

UTAH

WASHINGTON

WYOMING

SAN JOSÉ STATE UNIVERSITY

Address: One Washington Square, San José, CA 95192
Website: *https://www.sjsu.edu/design/animation-illustration/index.php*
Contact: *https://www.sjsu.edu/soar/about/contact-us.php*
Phone: (408) 283-7500
Email: admissions@sjsu.edu

COST OF ATTENDANCE:

In-State Tuition & Fees: $7,852 | **Additional Expenses:** $22,213
Total: $30,065

Out-of-State Tuition & Fees: $12,604 | **Additional Expenses:** $22,213
Total: $34,817

Financial Aid: https://www.sjsu.edu/faso/

ADDITIONAL INFORMATION:

Available Degree(s)

- BFA Animation & Illustration

Portfolio Requirement

Portfolios are not required for incoming students. They are required later in the program to ensure the student may move on to earn their BFA.

Scholarships Offered

SJSU is part of the California State University System, and offers campus, departmental, as well as private scholarships. Students are encouraged to submit applications for these scholarships.

Special Opportunities

Animation/Illustration students at SJSU host monthly seminars with high school-aged and younger students. Young students are encouraged to join one of the monthly SJSU tours to learn more about the program. High school students may get a tour of the facilities, look at samples of student works, and visit classrooms to learn about life as a student at SJSU.

Notable Alumni

Mary Blair, Gordon Smedt, and Michael Whelan

ALASKA

ARIZONA

CALIFORNIA

COLORADO

HAWAII

IDAHO

MONTANA

NEVADA

NEW MEXICO

OREGON

UTAH

WASHINGTON

WYOMING

WEST

ALASKA

ARIZONA

CALIFORNIA

COLORADO

HAWAII

IDAHO

MONTANA

NEVADA

NEW MEXICO

OREGON

UTAH

WASHINGTON

WYOMING

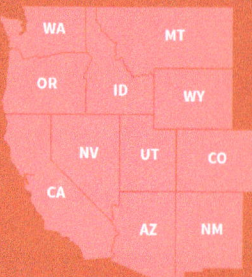

ROCKY MOUNTAIN COLLEGE OF ART AND DESIGN

Address: 1600 Pierce Street, Denver, CO, 80214
Website: *https://www.rmcad.edu/program/on-campus/illustration-school/*
Contact: *https://www.rmcad.edu/request-info/*
Phone: (303) 753-6046
Email: admissions@rmcad.edu

COST OF ATTENDANCE:

Tuition & Fees: $17,710 | **Additional Expenses:** $11,270
Total: $28,980

Financial Aid: https://www.rmcad.edu/admissions/financial-aid-tuition/financial-aid/

ADDITIONAL INFORMATION:

Available Degree(s)

- BFA Illustration

Portfolio Requirement

Portfolios are required for incoming students. Submit 10-15 works via SlideRoom.

Scholarships Offered

Incoming students with a GPA over 3.5 may earn an award of $360 per semester. RMCAD also offers Memorial, Presidential, and Best of Colorado Scholarships. They range from $1,700-$5,300 per semester.

Special Opportunities

There are three concentrations that illustration students may choose from: Children's Book, Concept Art, or Sequential Art. All illustration students learn visual storytelling, traditional and new media forms, composition theory, self promotion, portfolio development, and drawing mastery.

Notable Alumni

Lindsay Gruetzmacher, Phil Montaño, Jenny Morgan, and Paul Sullivan

UNIVERSITY OF COLORADO, DENVER

Address: 1201 Larimer St, Denver, CO 80204
Website: *https://artsandmedia.ucdenver.edu/areas-of-study/visual-arts/illustration*
Contact: *https://www.ucdenver.edu/about-cu-denver/contact-us*
Phone: (303) 315-2601
Email: admissions@ucdenver.edu

COST OF ATTENDANCE:

In-State Tuition & Fees: $9,228 | **Additional Expenses:** $18,198
Total: $27,426

Out-of-State Tuition & Fees: $24,924 | **Additional Expenses:** $18,198
Total: $43,122

Financial Aid: https://www.ucdenver.edu/student-finances/financial-aid

ADDITIONAL INFORMATION:

Available Degree(s)

- BFA Visual Arts, emphasis: Illustration

Portfolio Requirement

Portfolios are not required for incoming students. However, portfolio reviews are required after successful completion of first year coursework.

Scholarships Offered

Students may apply for CU Denver scholarships, which open every October. A FAFSA is required to be considered for need-based aid. Additionally, students may apply for scholarships through private donors through the ScholarLynx+ portal.

Special Opportunities

Illustration students take coursework such as digital painting, graphic novel design, typography, and anatomy for the artist. The BFA culminates in a senior thesis. By the time of graduation, students whill have built a strong portfolio of work that showcases their personal style.

Notable Alumni

Brandon Vargas, Travis Vermilye, and Patricia Walters

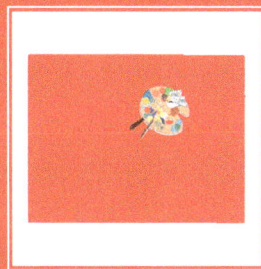

ALASKA

ARIZONA

CALIFORNIA

COLORADO

HAWAII

IDAHO

MONTANA

NEVADA

NEW MEXICO

OREGON

UTAH

WASHINGTON

WYOMING

WEST

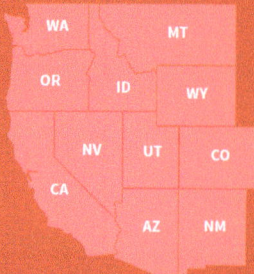

PACIFIC NORTHWEST COLLEGE OF ART

Address: 511 NW Broadway, Portland, OR 97209
Website: *https://pnca.edu/academics/bfa/illustration*
Contact: *https://pnca.edu/about/contact-hours*
Phone: (503) 226-4391
Email: pncaadmissions@willamette.edu

COST OF ATTENDANCE:

Tuition & Fees: $41,769 | **Additional Expenses:** $10,676
Total: $52,445

Financial Aid: https://pnca.edu/admissions/tuition-financial-aid/undergraduate

ADDITIONAL INFORMATION:

Available Degree(s)

- BFA Illustration

Portfolio Requirement

Portfolios are required for incoming students. Submit 10-15 works.

Scholarships Offered

Merit-based and need-based scholarships are offered at PNCA. Students are automatically considered for the Competitive Juried Scholarships, which is available to both U.S. citizens and international students. There are a handful of these scholarships, some of which give $10,000 per year. PNCA also offers equity scholarships toward students of color, ranging from $5,000 to full tuition per year.

Special Opportunities

Illustration students are trained to become skilled visual storytellers for a variety of fields, such as comic book publishing, visual journalism, surface design, animated films, computer gaming, and more. Traditional and alternative skills are emphasized alongside growth of visual communication skills.

Notable Alumni

Marlowe Dobbe, Morgaine Faye, Elana Gabrielle, Anke Gladnick, Samantha Mash, Molly Mendoza, Seaerra Miller, and Subin Yang

ALASKA

ARIZONA

CALIFORNIA

COLORADO

HAWAII

IDAHO

MONTANA

NEVADA

NEW MEXICO

OREGON

UTAH

WASHINGTON

WYOMING

BRIGHAM YOUNG UNIVERSITY

Address: Brigham Young University, Provo, UT 84602
Website: *https://designdept.byu.edu/illustration*
Contact: https://enrollment.byu.edu/enrollment-services-counselors
Phone: (801) 422-4104
Email: admissions@byu.edu

COST OF ATTENDANCE:

Tuition & Fees: $12,240 | **Additional Expenses:** $14,036
Total: $26,276

*Note: BYU is affiliated with the Church of Jesus Christ of Latter-day Saints. Students who are affiliated with the Church have lower costs (Tuition: $6,120, COA: $20,156).

Financial Aid: https://enrollment.byu.edu/financialaid

ADDITIONAL INFORMATION:

Available Degree(s)

- BFA Illustration

Portfolio Requirement

Portfolios are not required for incoming students. Students enter as a pre-major, then a pre-BFA, then a full BFA major. They must pass a series of portfolio reviews to earn the full BFA.

Scholarships Offered

Freshman scholarships are merit-based and include the Russell M. Nelson Scholarship (150% of Latter-day Saints Tuition for 8 semesters), the Sterling Scholarship Competition (for UT high school seniors), and the National Merit Scholarship (for National Merit finalists). In addition, international students are eligible for academic, merit-based scholarships.

Special Opportunities

BYU illustration students are prepared for competitive and evolving markets. Students have opportunities to participate in conferences, study abroad, internships, and field trips. Students are also required to complete a capstone project that incorporates research, writing, history, presentation, and business. They later present their work in a physical space, such as the Harris Fine Arts Center.

Notable Alumni

Joseph F. Brickey, Martin D. Havran, Brett L. Helquist, and David R. McClellan

ALASKA

ARIZONA

CALIFORNIA

COLORADO

HAWAII

IDAHO

MONTANA

NEVADA

NEW MEXICO

OREGON

UTAH

WASHINGTON

WYOMING

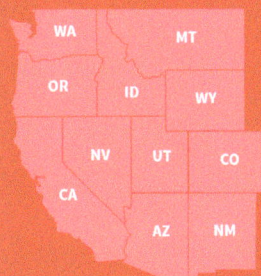

WEST

CHAPTER 15

ILLUSTRATION AND COMIC BOOK PROGRAMS BY CITY/ STATE

School	City	State
University of Arizona	Tuscon	Arizona
California State University, Fullerton (CSUF)	Fullerton	California
Laguna College of Art and Design	Laguna Beach	California
California State University, Long Beach	Long Beach	California
Otis College of Art and Design	Los Angeles	California
California State University, Northridge (CSUN)	Northridge	California
ArtCenter College of Design	Pasadena	California
Academy of Art University	San Francisco	California
California College of the Arts	San Francisco	California
San José State University (SJSU)	San José	California
Rocky Mountain College of Art and Design	Denver	Colorado
University of Colorado, Denver	Denver	Colorado
University of Connecticut (UConn)	Storrs	Connecticut
University of Hartford	West Hartford	Connecticut
University of Central Florida	Orlando	Florida
Ringling College of Art and Design	Sarasota	Florida
University of Georgia	Athens	Georgia
Savannah College of Art and Design	Savannah	Georgia
Columbia College Chicago	Chicago	Illinois
School of the Art Institute Chicago	Chicago	Illinois
Purdue University	West Lafayette	Indiana
Maine College of Art & Design	Portland	Maine
Maryland Institute College of Art	Baltimore	Maryland
Massachusetts College of Art & Design	Boston	Massachusetts
Ferris State University	Big Rapids	Michigan
College for Creative Studies	Detroit	Michigan
Minneapolis College of Art & Design	Minneapolis	Minnesota
Kansas City Art Institute	Kansas City	Missouri
Washington University, St. Louis	St. Louis	Missouri
Pratt Institute	Brooklyn	New York
Fashion Institute of Technology	New York	New York
Parsons School of Design	New York	New York
School of Visual Arts	New York	New York
Rochester Institute of Technology	Rochester	New York
Syracuse University	Syracuse	New York
University of North Carolina at Charlotte	Charlotte	North Carolina

School	City	State
East Carolina University	Greenville	North Carolina
Art Academy of Cincinnati	Cincinnati	Ohio
Cleveland Institute of Art	Cleveland	Ohio
Columbus College of Art & Design	Columbus	Ohio
Pacific Northwest College of Art	Portland	Oregon
Pennsylvania Academy of Fine Arts (PAFA) + University of Pennsylvania	Philadelphia	Pennsylvania
University of the Arts	Philadelphia	Pennsylvania
Rhode Island School of Design	Providence	Rhode Island
Belmont University	Nashville	Tennessee
Texas State University	San Marcos	Texas
Brigham Young University	Provo	Utah
Virginia Commonwealth University	Richmond	Virginia
Milwaukee Institute of Art & Design	Milwaukee	Wisconsin

CHAPTER 16

ILLUSTRATION AND COMIC BOOK PROGRAMS BY AVERAGE TEST SCORE

ILLUSTRATION AND COMIC BOOK PROGRAMS BY AVERAGE SAT

School	Avg. SAT
California State University, Northridge (CSUN)	460-560 (ERW) 440-550 (M)
Ferris State University	470-580 (ERW) 470-580 (M)
University of Colorado, Denver	490-610 (ERW) 510-600 (M)
California State University, Fullerton (CSUF)	500-590 (ERW) 500-590 (M)
San José State University (SJSU)	500-640 (ERW) 520-680 (M)
East Carolina University	510-590 (ERW) 510-580 (M)
Texas State University	510-600 (ERW) 500-580 (M)
University of Hartford	510-610 (ERW) 510-600 (M)
California State University, Long Beach	510-620 (ERW) 510-620 (M)
Savannah College of Art and Design	540-640 (ERW) 500-600 (M)
Virginia Commonwealth University	540-640 (ERW) 520-610 (M)
School of Visual Arts	545-650 (ERW) 530-680 (M)
University of Arizona	550-660 (ERW) 540-690 (M)
University of North Carolina at Charlotte	560-640 (ERW) 560-640 (M)
School of the Art Institute Chicago	560-660 (ERW) 480-600 (M)
Cleveland Institute of Art	560-680 (ERW) 510-620 (M)
Pratt Institute	570-660 (ERW) 550-680 (M)
Belmont University	580-660 (ERW) 540-640 (M)
Parsons School of Design	580-680 (ERW) 560-680 (M)
University of Connecticut (UConn)	580-680 (ERW) 590-710 (M)
Purdue University	590-690 (ERW) 600-740 (M)
University of Central Florida	600-680 (ERW) 570-670 (M)
Rochester Institute of Technology	600-690 (ERW) 620-730 (M)
Rhode Island School of Design	610-700 (ERW) 640-770 (M)
Brigham Young University	610-700 (ERW) 590-710 (M)
University of Georgia	620-700 (ERW) 600-720 (M)
Washington University, St. Louis	720-760 (ERW) 760-800 (M)
Syracuse University	N/A
College for Creative Studies	N/A *Not required
Academy of Art University	N/A *Open admissions
Art Academy of Cincinnati	N/A *Test optional
ArtCenter College of Design	N/A *Test optional
California College of the Arts	N/A *Test optional
Columbia College Chicago	N/A *Test optional
Columbus College of Art & Design	N/A *Test optional
Fashion Institute of Technology	N/A *Test optional

School	Avg. SAT
Kansas City Art Institute	N/A *Test optional
Laguna College of Art and Design	N/A *Test optional
Maine College of Art & Design	N/A *Test optional
Maryland Institute College of Art	N/A *Test optional
Massachusetts College of Art & Design	N/A *Test optional
Milwaukee Institute of Art & Design	N/A *Test optional
Minneapolis College of Art & Design	N/A *Test optional
Otis College of Art and Design	N/A *Test optional
Pacific Northwest College of Art	N/A *Test optional
Pennsylvania Academy of Fine Arts (PAFA) + University of Pennsylvania	N/A *Test optional
Ringling College of Art and Design	N/A *Test optional
Rocky Mountain College of Art and Design	N/A *Test optional
University of the Arts	N/A *Test optional

ILLUSTRATION AND COMIC BOOK PROGRAMS BY AVERAGE ACT

School	Avg. ACT C
California State University, Northridge (CSUN)	16-22
California State University, Fullerton (CSUF)	18-23
Ferris State University	18-26
East Carolina University	19-24
Cleveland Institute of Art	19-27
Texas State University	20-25
California State University, Long Beach	20-26
Savannah College of Art and Design	20-27
San José State University (SJSU)	20-31
Virginia Commonwealth University	21-28
University of Arizona	21-29
School of the Art Institute Chicago	22-25
University of Colorado, Denver	22-27
University of North Carolina at Charlotte	22-27
University of Hartford	22-29
School of Visual Arts	23-27
Belmont University	23-30
Pratt Institute	25-30
University of Central Florida	25-30
Purdue University	25-33

School	Avg. ACT C
Parsons School of Design	26-30
Brigham Young University	26-32
Rhode Island School of Design	27-32
University of Connecticut (UConn)	27-32
University of Georgia	27-32
Rochester Institute of Technology	28-33
Washington University, St. Louis	33-35
Syracuse University	N/A
College for Creative Studies	N/A *Not required
Academy of Art University	N/A *Open admissions
Art Academy of Cincinnati	N/A *Test optional
ArtCenter College of Design	N/A *Test optional
California College of the Arts	N/A *Test optional
Columbia College Chicago	N/A *Test optional
Columbus College of Art & Design	N/A *Test optional
Fashion Institute of Technology	N/A *Test optional
Kansas City Art Institute	N/A *Test optional
Laguna College of Art and Design	N/A *Test optional
Maine College of Art & Design	N/A *Test optional
Maryland Institute College of Art	N/A *Test optional
Massachusetts College of Art & Design	N/A *Test optional
Milwaukee Institute of Art & Design	N/A *Test optional
Minneapolis College of Art & Design	N/A *Test optional
Otis College of Art and Design	N/A *Test optional
Pacific Northwest College of Art	N/A *Test optional
Pennsylvania Academy of Fine Arts (PAFA) + University of Pennsylvania	N/A *Test optional
Ringling College of Art and Design	N/A *Test optional
Rocky Mountain College of Art and Design	N/A *Test optional
University of the Arts	N/A *Test optional

ILLUSTRATION AND COMIC BOOK PROGRAMS BY AVERAGE GPA

School	Avg. GPA
Otis College of Art and Design	3.26
East Carolina University	3.28
Ferris State University	3.32
California State University, Northridge (CSUN)	3.39
University of Arizona	3.43
Savannah College of Art and Design	3.6
Purdue University	3.67
Syracuse University	3.67
Rochester Institute of Technology	3.7
Virginia Commonwealth University	3.72
Pratt Institute	3.82
Belmont University	3.83
University of North Carolina at Charlotte	3.92
University of Georgia	4.02
Washington University, St. Louis	4.21
California State University, Long Beach	3.68
Brigham Young University	3.86
University of Central Florida	4.16
Art Academy of Cincinnati	N/A
ArtCenter College of Design	N/A
California College of the Arts	N/A
California State University, Fullerton (CSUF)	N/A
Cleveland Institute of Art	N/A
College for Creative Studies	N/A
Columbia College Chicago	N/A
Columbus College of Art & Design	N/A
Fashion Institute of Technology	N/A
Kansas City Art Institute	N/A
Laguna College of Art and Design	N/A
Maine College of Art & Design	N/A
Maryland Institute College of Art	N/A
Massachusetts College of Art & Design	N/A
Milwaukee Institute of Art & Design	N/A
Minneapolis College of Art & Design	N/A
Pacific Northwest College of Art	N/A
Parsons School of Design	N/A

School	Avg. GPA
Pennsylvania Academy of Fine Arts (PAFA) + University of Pennsylvania	N/A
Rhode Island School of Design	N/A
Ringling College of Art and Design	N/A
Rocky Mountain College of Art and Design	N/A
San José State University (SJSU)	N/A
School of the Art Institute Chicago	N/A
School of Visual Arts	N/A
Texas State University	N/A
University of Colorado, Denver	N/A
University of Connecticut (UConn)	N/A
University of Hartford	N/A
University of the Arts	N/A
Academy of Art University	N/A *Open admissions

CHAPTER 17

LEADING ILLUSTRATION, COMIC BOOK DESIGN, PAINTING, & FINE ARTS PROGRAMS

TOP UNDERGRADUATE SCHOOLS IN ILLUSTRATION

1. Rhode Island School of Design
2. Syracuse University
3. ArtCenter College of Design
4. Fashion Institute of Technology
5. College of Creative Studies
6. Pratt Institute
7. Rochester Inst. of Tech.
8. Maryland Institute College of Art
9. Brigham Young University
10. Virginia Commonwealth University

TOP 50 UNDERGRADUATE AND GRADUATE SCHOOLS IN ILLUSTRATION (ACCORDING TO ANIMATION CAREER REVIEW)

1. School of Visual Arts
2. ArtCenter College of Design
3. Rhode Island School of Design
4. Ringling College of Art & Design
5. Savannah College of Art & Design
6. Pratt Institute
7. Maryland Institute College of Art
8. California College of the Arts
9. Parsons School of Design
10. Otis College of Art & Design
11. Fashion Institute of Technology
12. Minneapolis College of Art & Design
13. Massachusetts College of Art & Design
14. Columbus College of Art & Design
15. College for Creative Studies
16. Kansas City Art Institute
17. Virginia Commonwealth
18. Syracuse University
19. San Jose State University
20. Cleveland Institute of Art
21. Laguna College of Art & Design
22. California State University, Fullerton
23. Washington University in St. Louis
24. Academy of Art University
25. Brigham Young University
26. California State University, Long Beach
27. Pacific Northwest College of Art
28. Milwaukee Institute of Art & Design
29. University of Central Florida
30. California State University, Northridge
31. Rocky Mountain College of Art & Design
32. University of the Arts
33. Columbia College Chicago
34. Ferris State University
35. Rochester Inst. of Tech.
36. Indiana University – Purdue
37. University of Georgia
38. Texas State University, San Marcos
39. University of Colorado, Denver

40. University of North Carolina, Charlotte
41. University of Connecticut
42. University of Arizona
43. East Carolina University
44. Belmont University
45. University of Illinois at Chicago
46. UPenn + Pennsylvania Academy of Fine Arts
47. University of Miami
48. Maine College of Art
49. Art Academy of Cincinnati
50. University of Hartford

TOP SIXTEEN PAINTING PROGRAMS

1. Yale University
2. Rhode Island School of Design
3. School of the Art Institute of Chicago
4. Columbia University
5. Bard College
6. Boston University
7. Maryland Institute College of Art
8. UCLA
9. California Institute of the Arts
10. Hunter College - CUNY
11. Pratt Institute
12. School of Visual Arts
13. Virginia Commonwealth University
14. Cranbrook Academy of Art
15. Temple University
16. Rutgers University

COLLEGES OFFERING THE MOST BACHELOR'S DEGREES IN FINE ART EACH YEAR

1. School of the Art Institute of Chicago
2. California State University, Fullerton
3. California State University, Long Beach
4. University of North Texas
5. City University of New York
6. Florida State University
7. University of Central Florida
8. San Jose State University
9. Indiana University – Purdue
10. Hunter College - CUNY

CHAPTER 18

TOP U.S. & INTERNATIONAL ART PROGRAMS

U.S. – ACCREDITED COLLEGES FOCUSED ON ART

United States

Art Academy of Cincinnati (OH)

ArtCenter College of Design (CA)

Art Institute of Boston (MA)

Art Institute of Pittsburgh (PA)

California College of the Arts (CA)

California Institute of the Arts (CA)

Cleveland Institute of Art (OH)

College for Creative Studies (MI)

Columbia College Chicago (IL)

Cooper Union (NY)

Corcoran Col. of Art & Design - GWU (DC)

Cornish College of the Arts (WA)

Fashion Institute of Technology (NY)

Kansas City Art Institute (MO)

Kendall College of Art & Design (MI)

Laguna College of Art & Design (CA)

Lyme Academy College of Fine Arts (CT)

Maine College of Art (ME)

Maryland Institute College of Art (MD)

Mass. College of Art & Design (MA)

Memphis College of Art (TN)

Milwaukee Institute of Art & Design (WI)

Minneapolis College of Art & Design (MN)

Montserrat College of Art (MA)

Moore College of Art & Design (PA)

New Hampshire Institute of Art (NH)

N. Mich. Univ. School of Art & Design (MI)

Oregon College of Art & Craft (OR)

Otis College of Art & Design (CA)

Pacific Northwest College of Art (OR)

Parsons School of Design (NY)

Pratt Institute (NY)

Rhode Island School of Design (RI)

Ringling College of Art & Design (FL)

San Francisco Art Institute (CA)

Savannah College of Art & Design (GA)

School of the Art Institute of Chicago (IL)

School of the Museum of Fine Arts (MA)

Vermont College of Fine Arts (VT)

Watkins College of Art, Design, & Film (TN)

U.S. – ACCREDITED COLLEGES FOCUSED ON ART

International

Adelaide Central School of Art (Australia)

Alberta University of the Arts (Canada)

Bauhaus University Weimar (Germany)

Camberwell College of Arts (England)

Emily Carr Univ. of Art & Design (Canada)

Government College of Art & Craft (India)

Grekov Odessa Art School (Ukraine)

National Art School (Australia)

Nova Scotia College of Art & Design Univ. (Canada)

Ontario College of Art & Design Univ. (Canada)

Paris College of Art (France)

2021 QS RANKED TOP UNIVERSITIES FOR ART AND DESIGN WORLDWIDE

1. Royal College of Art (U.K.)
2. University of the Arts London (U.K.)
3. Parsons School of Design (NY-USA)
4. Rhode Island School of Design (RI-USA)
5. Massachusetts Institute of Technology (MA-USA)
6. Politecnico de Milano (Italy)
7. Aalto University (Finland)
8. School of the Art Institute of Chicago (IL-USA)
9. Glasgow School of Art (U.K.)
10. Pratt Institute (NY-USA)
11. ArtCenter (CA-USA)
12. Delft University of Technology (Netherlands)
13. Design Academy Eindhoven (Netherlands)
14. Tongji University (China)
15. Goldsmiths, University of London (U.K.)
16. Royal Melbourne Institute of Technology (Australia)
17. California Institute of the Arts (CA-USA)
18. Carnegie Mellon University (PA-USA)
19. Stanford University (CA-USA)
20. Hong Kong Polytechnic University (H.K. SAR)

LIVE YOUR LIFE WITH INTENTION. LIVE THE LIFE YOU'VE ALWAYS DREAMED OF; THE LIFE YOU HAVE ALWAYS IMAGINED LIVING.

JOURNEY TO ART, DANCE, MUSIC, THEATRE, FILM, AND FASHION SERIES

JOURNEY TO
Fashion Design
COLLEGE ADMISSIONS & PROFILES

RACHEL A. WINSTON, PH.D.

JOURNEY TO
Fashion Merchandising
COLLEGE ADMISSIONS & PROFILES

RACHEL A. WINSTON, PH.D.

JOURNEY TO
Costume Design & Technical Theatre
COLLEGE ADMISSIONS & PROFILES

RACHEL A. WINSTON, PH.D.

JOURNEY TO
Theatre and the Dramatic Arts
COLLEGE ADMISSIONS & PROFILES

STAGE DOOR

RACHEL A. WINSTON, PH.D.

Live your dreams today remembering that discipline is the bridge between dreams and achievement!

"We believe in the American Dream that all people rich or poor can go as far in life as their talents and persistence will take them."
– Lizard Publishing Vision

At Lizard, we help you make your dreams come true.

CONTACT INFORMATION

Phone: 949-833-7706
E-mail: collegeguide@yahoo.com
Website: collegelizard.com and Lizard-publishing.com

COMPREHENSIVE HEALTH CARE SERIES

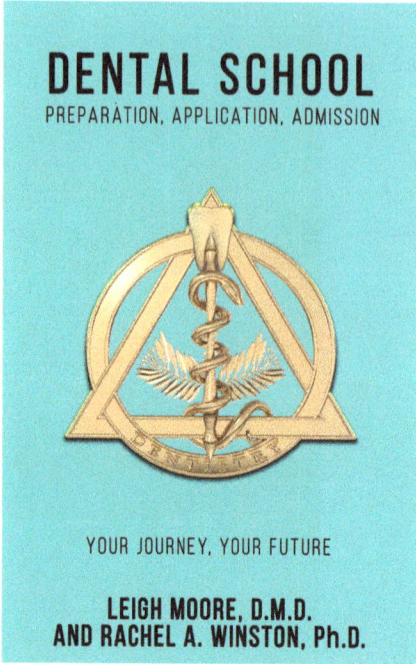

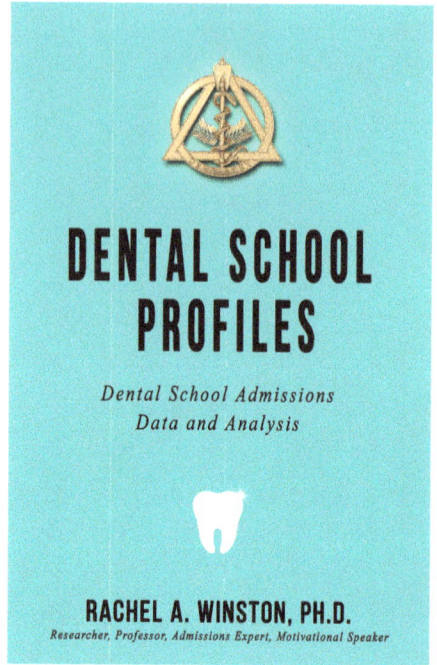

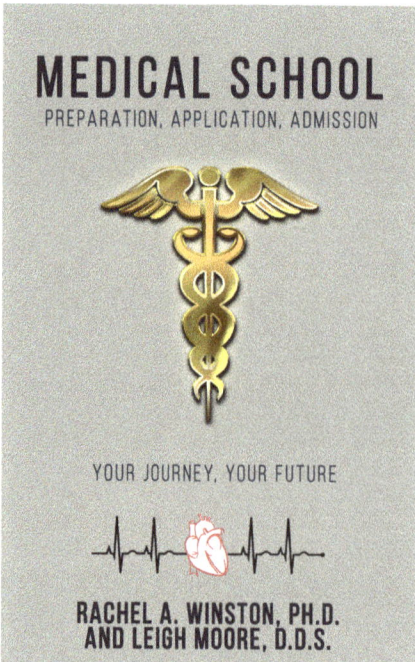

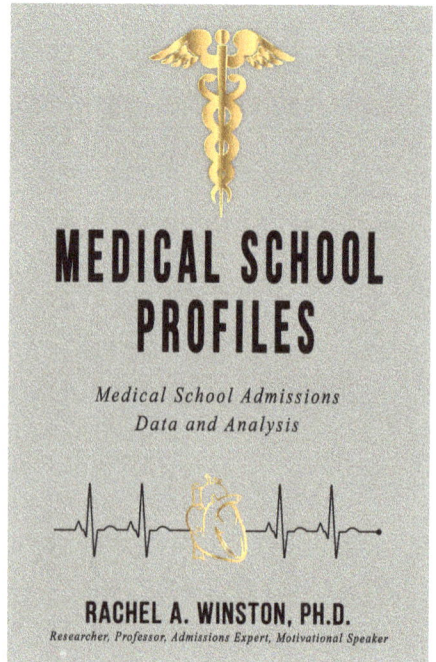

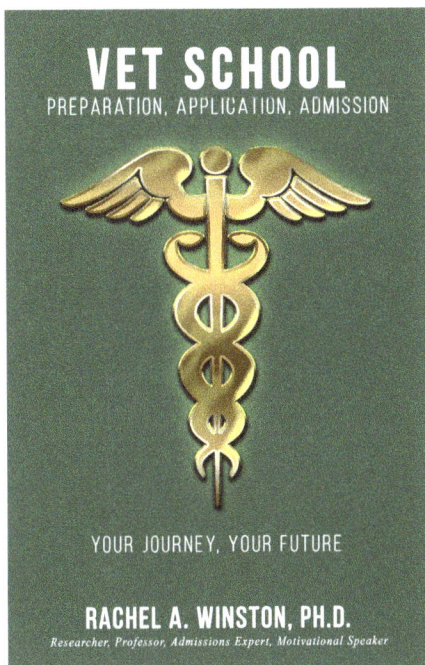

VET SCHOOL
PREPARATION, APPLICATION, ADMISSION

YOUR JOURNEY, YOUR FUTURE

RACHEL A. WINSTON, PH.D.
Researcher, Professor, Admissions Expert, Motivational Speaker

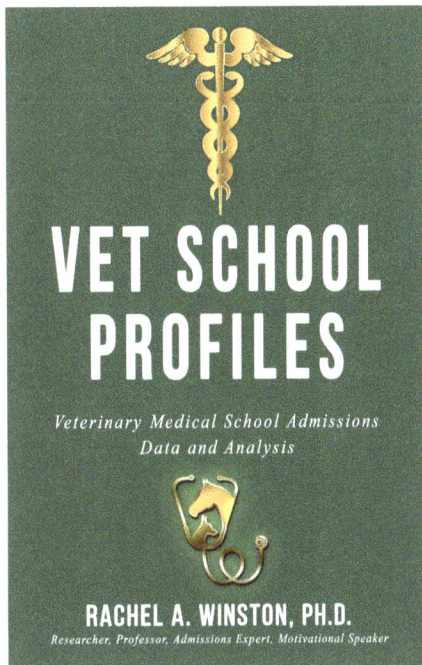

VET SCHOOL PROFILES

Veterinary Medical School Admissions Data and Analysis

RACHEL A. WINSTON, PH.D.
Researcher, Professor, Admissions Expert, Motivational Speaker

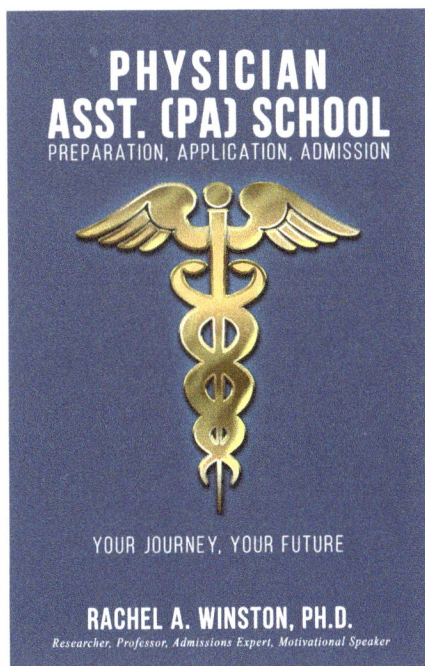

PHYSICIAN ASST. (PA) SCHOOL
PREPARATION, APPLICATION, ADMISSION

YOUR JOURNEY, YOUR FUTURE

RACHEL A. WINSTON, PH.D.
Researcher, Professor, Admissions Expert, Motivational Speaker

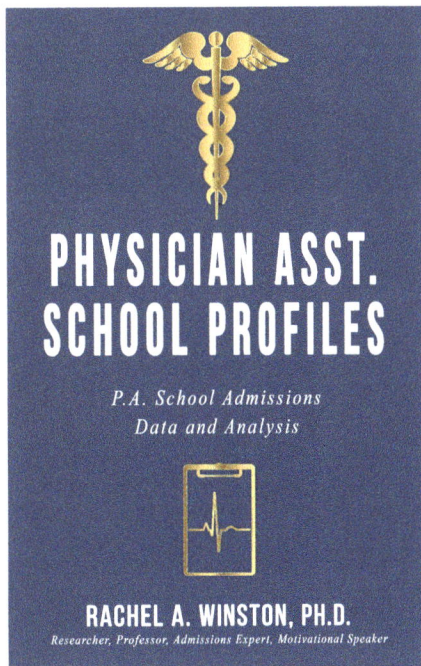

PHYSICIAN ASST. SCHOOL PROFILES

P.A. School Admissions Data and Analysis

RACHEL A. WINSTON, PH.D.
Researcher, Professor, Admissions Expert, Motivational Speaker

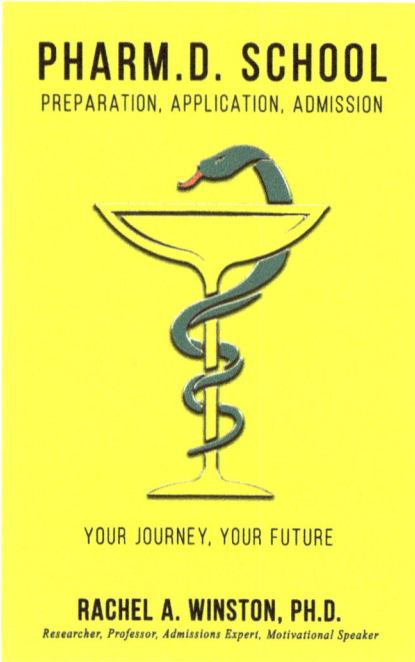

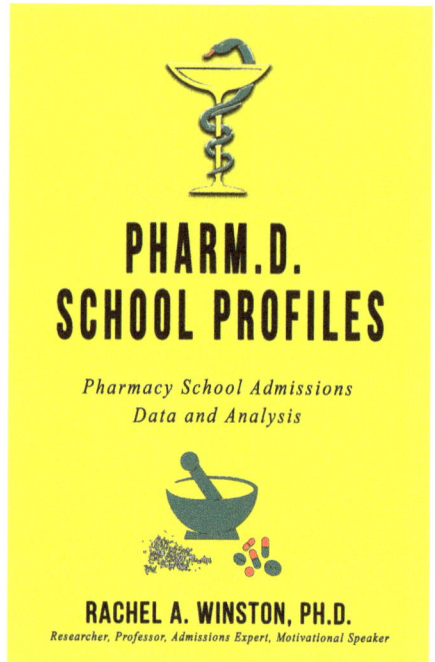

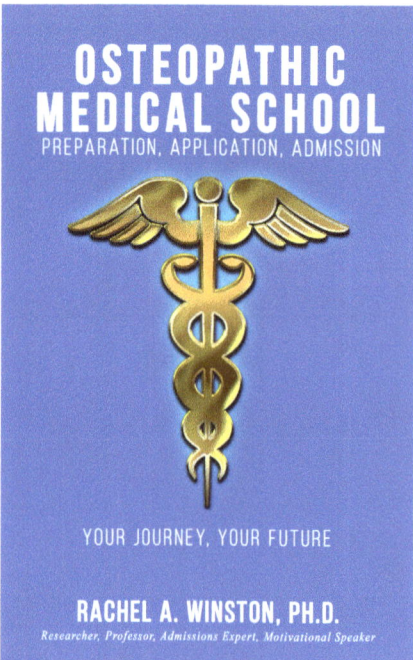

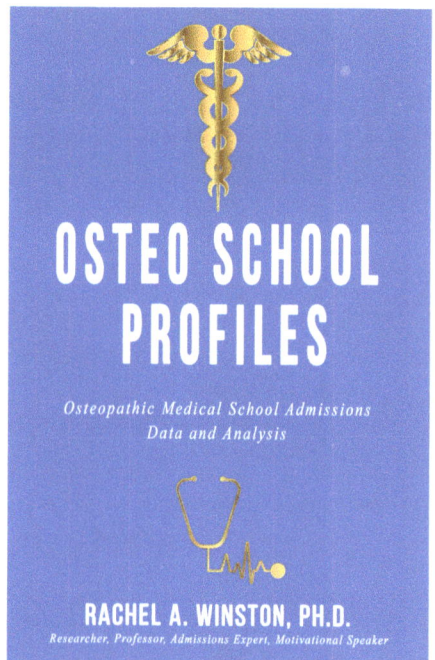

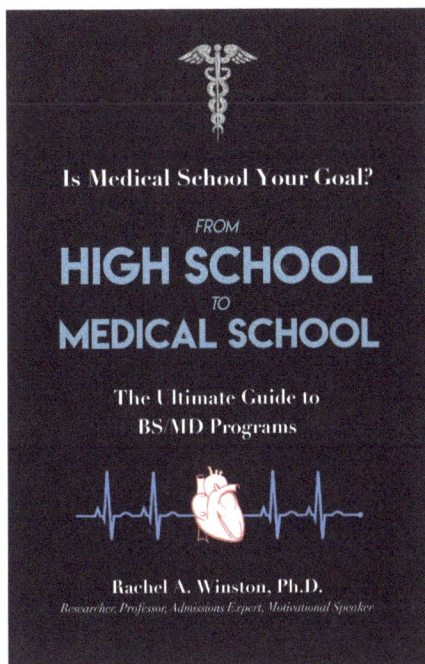

This comprehensive healthcare series is designed in full color to aid the growing number of applicants seeking clear, comprehensive materials. As a college admissions expert and former UCLA College Counseling Certificate Program faculty member, Dr. Winston is dedicated to helping students obtain the information they need.

FOR MORE INFORMATION

bsmdguide.com

medschoolexpert.com

Purchase books at Lizard-publishing.com

Is Medical School Your Goal?

FROM

HIGH SCHOOL
TO
MEDICAL SCHOOL

The Ultimate Guide to
BS/MD Programs

Rachel A. Winston, Ph.D.
Researcher, Professor, Admissions Expert, Motivational Speaker

SERVICES OFFERED BY LIZARD EDUCATION:

- College Counseling
- Admissions News/Resources
- Essay Support and Editing
- Interview Preparation
- Road Trips to Visit Colleges
- Career Planning/Majors/ Resumes
- BS/MD, BS/DO, BS/JD, BS/DDS
- Medical School
- Graduate School (Masters & Doctorate)

- Film Studio and Editing
- Portfolio Assistance/SlideRoom
- Athletics Recruiting/Highlight Films
- International Admissions/Visa/ TOEFL
- Financial Aid and Scholarships
- UCs, Ivy Leagues, and Colleges Nationwide
- Book Publishing
- Engineering, Robotics, STEM
- Art Portfolios

Email: collegeguide@yahoo.com

Website: collegelizard.com

LIZARD

INDEX

Symbols

A

B

C

D

E

F

G

H

I

N

O

P

R

S

T

U

V

W

Y

Z

www.ingramcontent.com/pod-product-compliance
Lightning Source LLC
Chambersburg PA
CBHW041936260326
41914CB00010B/1315